T0101022

THE
CAPITAL
ONE
STORY

How the Upstart Financial Institution
Charged Toward Market Leadership

Published by HarperCollins Leadership, an imprint of HarperCollins Focus LLC.

Published in association with Kevin Anderson & Associates: https://www.ka-writing.com/.

Book design by Aubrey Khan, Neuwirth & Associates.

ISBN 978-1-4002-1872-1 (eBook)
ISBN 978-1-4002-1871-4 (HC)

Library of Congress Control Number: 2020931342

Printed in the United States of America
20 21 22 23 LSC 10 9 8 7 6 5 4 3 2 1

CONTENTS

AUTHOR'S NOTE

Capital One declined all interviews and participation in this venture. All interviews and quotes come directly from online presentations, news articles, books, case studies, as well as Capital One's website, annual reports, and press releases.

"Credit cards aren't banking—
they're information."

—RICHARD FAIRBANK,
Founder and CEO, Capital One

1994

Signet Financial Corp announces the corporate spin-off of its credit card division, naming Richard Fairbank as CEO and Nigel Morris as President and COO.

1998

Capital One expands into auto loans by acquiring auto financing company Summit Acceptance Corporation.

1999

CEO Richard Fairbank announces move to use Capital One's experience with collecting consumer data to offer loans, insurance, and phone service.

2000

"What's in your wallet?" tagline debuts.

2002

Capital One and the US Postal Service propose a negotiated services agreement for bulk discount in mailing services.

2003

The Florida Citrus Bowl is rebranded the Capital One Bowl and sponsors a mascot challenge every year, announcing the winner on the day of the Capital One Bowl.

2019

Capital One launches a budgeting app for consumers called ENO.

2019

Capital One discovers unauthorized access on their Amazon Web Service–hosted platform by one individual responsible for compromising 106 million people in both the United States and Canada combined. The FBI is immediately notified.

2017

Capital One exits the mortgage origination business and lays off 1,100 employees.

2015

Capital One acquires General Electric's Healthcare Financial Services unit.

2012

Capital One acquires ING Direct and rebrands the company as Capital One 360.

2009

Capital One repurchases company stock issued to the US Treasury for $3.67 billion, resulting in a profit of more than $100 million to the US Treasury.

2007

Capital One acquires NetSpend, a marketer of prepaid debit cards.

I t's impossible to go a day without seeing or hearing mention of Capital One. Their witty, star-studded commercials and print ads are ubiquitous. Though relatively new to the banking and credit industry compared to their historic competitors, they have been steadily growing and edging out the competition for the past twenty-five years. They're growing so much they are now one of the top 10 credit issuers, keeping company with some of the most enduring banks in US history. Capital One is not just enduring but historic and groundbreaking as well. It's hard to imagine that such a new company could have anything in common with the legacy banks, but in fact, they do.

A Very Brief History of US Banking and Lending

Some names are synonymous with banking—BNY Mellon and JPMorgan Chase for example. Some with history. Some are synonymous with both. Enjoying a resurge in popularity thanks in large part to the smash hit *Hamilton*, founding fathers Aaron Burr and Alexander Hamilton are some such names. Though the two are well-known frenemies and helped shape our nation, what is little known, however, is that the two rivals are also the founders of two of the largest and longest-enduring US banks. While we tend to think of "Big Banks" as something unique to our age, they have been part of the fabric of American life since its inception.

It's All About the Hamiltons

One of the US's oldest banks, The Bank of New York, was founded by none other than Alexander Hamilton himself in 1784. Upon his return from serving in Congress, Hamilton returned to New York and saw a business opportunity—credit. Merchants in the growing city needed access to credit in order to finance their new business ventures. However, there was one segment of the business population Hamilton refused to lend to—his enemies, the Jeffersonian Republicans—which essentially amounted to half of the merchants in New York.

Enter Hamilton's long-time rival, Aaron Burr. Not to be outdone, Aaron Burr, who had been outspokenly anti-Federalist and anti-credit, in a bold (and some might even argue devious) move reworded some language in a charter that had been created to build a private water company for New Yorkers. In the newly worded charter, Burr made a provision that the water company could accept deposits and make loans. In essence the Manhattan Water Co. was a bank—or what became known as the Manhattan Bank. Burr could now lend to his peers who had been shut out previously by Hamilton and his Federalist friends. With this new influx in money and access, the entire political and financial landscape changed in America.

Some historians, like Robert E. Wright, author of *One Nation Under Debt: Hamilton, Jefferson, and the History of What We Owe,* argues it's the reason Jefferson was even elected president in 1800.[1] With the new infusion of cash flow, he had access to otherwise inaccessible funds thanks to Burr's Manhattan Bank. Money playing a role in politics, it appears, is as old as America itself. Similarly, shutting people out of credit and discriminating against them (and finding ways to bypass discrimination) has been as well.

> In fact, nine out of the ten largest banks in the US have been around for more than 100 years. They have survived forty-seven recessions, stock market crashes, an ensuing Depression, Democratic and Republican presidencies, a Civil War, two World Wars, countless other wars, mergers, acquisitions, and even Ponzi schemes.

Though the times have certainly changed, banking and the rivalries among banks have remained largely the same. Hamilton's Bank of New York still survives today, though it is known as New York Mellon (BNY having merged with Mellon in 2006). Similarly, Burr's Manhattan bank survives as JPMorgan Chase, (having first merged with Chase and then JPMorgan in 2000). To this day, our founding fathers' banks, JPMorgan Chase and Mellon endure and are on the Top 10 list of largest banks in the US.[2] In fact, nine out of the ten largest banks in the US have been around for more than 100 years. They have survived forty-seven recessions,[3] stock market crashes, an ensuing Depression, Democratic and Republican presidencies, a Civil War, two World Wars, countless other wars, mergers, acquisitions, and even Ponzi schemes. These old banks and the leaders that founded them, have been, for better or for worse, part of the continuing unfolding American story.

Capital One's Origin Story

Among these top ten largest US banks (by assets), however, one bank stands out precisely because it *hasn't* shared in this rich and complex past. Though it is only twenty-five years old, Capital One is no less a part of the ever unfolding American story—and more accurately—its future. Its origin story, ironically, comes about for reasons very similar to why the two oldest and largest began in the first place: The consumers' need for access to credit and the founders of the bank's desire to bypass discrimination.

Capital One, though fairly new, is linked intrinsically to both American spirit and history. Its founders also share many striking similarities to US banking's early founders. Fairbank, like Burr, is American-born, and Morris, like Hamilton, is an immigrant. When they founded Capital One, the two were young visionaries who saw consumer needs changing and were ready to seize the opportunity. Like Burr, they saw that only half of all Americans at the time had access to credit and they sought to democratize the process. Like Hamilton, they wanted to bring America into a modern era, where it could both prosper and grow and meet the demands of a changing socioeconomic, political, and rapidly developing landscape. But, unlike Burr and Hamilton, the two won't be meeting in a duel on a field in New Jersey anytime soon. To this day, they remain friends and leaders and in the banking and FinTech (the area of where financial services and digital technology meet) industries. Unlike any other large bank on the Top Ten List, Capital One's founder still sits in the CEO chair and commands the vision of the bank itself.

> ❝❝ Capital One, though fairly new, is linked intrinsically to both American spirit and history.

Banking Reimagined

In the past two decades, Capital One has enjoyed not just a meteoric rise in the financial industry, but in US business as a whole, specifically in the FinTech industry. From its start, Capital One has been shaking up the old, storied banking industry and brought new and innovative practices that have changed how people bank and understand their relationship with what was in their wallet. Robert Alexander, Capital One's CIO, who has served in various capacities over his 20-year tenure with the company is well aware of advantages of being the relative new kid on the block. One of the key advantages is having a mindset focused on innovation and technology from the outset. "Our products are just ephemeral products. It is principally software and data. Yes, we have branches, and yes, we have pieces of plastic that you put in your wallet today, though some people just carry them on their phone as digital versions of that. Our products though are intangible products, and so at the core of our business is the important role that technology plays, and it is about software, and it is about data and analytics, and it is about how you bring all of that together to create a great experience for customers."[4]

Alexander, and by extension, Capital One as a bank, recognize this is where the financial world is going and has been going for the past two decades. Gone are the days of safe deposit boxes, ledgers, and, in some cases, bank tellers or even ATMs. Instead, Capital One's primary focus has been on a digital strategic realization. Alexander credits this vision to Fairbank. "Our whole executive team is aligned around this view that we need to be technology leaders and digital leaders in our industry to win," Alexander says. And by win he means become the leader in *almost every segment* in banking, not just credit cards. Though Capital One started as a monoline credit card company—with no savings accounts, no checking accounts, no safe deposit boxes or branches, it is currently active in numerous segments of commercial banking. "We have a mix of products and a mix of customers that are more slanted toward digital than other large financial institutions. We are one of a short list of institutions that have a national footprint, so that we can build a national brand on the back of a credit card, on the back of our digital bank, as well as other businesses. We have a great positioning strategically on multiple dimensions," Alexander continues.[5]

The strategy Alexander speaks of dates back to the start of the bank itself. Morris and Fairbank met while working at a consultancy firm. Fairbank hired Morris just out of business school. Some of their assignments at the firm required that they work with historic, large New York banking institutions. While working with a legacy bank, Fairbank began to see patterns—the most profitable parts of the banks were their credit card lines, and yet no one seemed to be paying attention to them. Rather, the bankers' focus was on investments or other financial services. No one was looking at the data, and the data was telling both Morris and Fairbank that credit was both profitable, and an untapped market. At the time only 55 percent of Americans had access to credit.[6] Determined to change how banks do business and help consumers have access to credit, Fairbank, with the help of his friend Morris, ultimately transformed the modern banking industry that had withstood the winds of change for more than two-hundred years.

United by their vision for a new kind of banking and determined to bring banking into the 20th and then 21st centuries based on real data, Morris and Fairbank launched a new type of bank in 1994 and with it a new way for Americans to engage in business, trade, build credit, create wealth, and ultimately, as the nation's founders intended, pursue happiness.

What to Expect in This Book

In this book you will find out how Fairbank took his vision for a new kind of banking and created a different kind of bank, a "fair bank" if you will, one that America had not seen before. You will learn how he and Morris overcame early obstacles, both personal and professional, and how they eventually disrupted a historic and slow-to-change, Big-Bank dominated industry and you'll learn the tactics they used to quickly dominate the market. You'll learn how they were one of the first banks in the world to use consumer data and research to look for trends in the marketplace. You'll also find out how they dealt with pitfalls and major challenges, like the subprime mortgage crisis and the crash of 2008. Every young company has to learn to withstand the inevitable learning curves and growing pains— and Capital One did so and is still standing. They dealt with internal and external turmoil, politics, and the changing landscape of banking—especially as it related to online banking and ongoing technological innovations.

Over the past decade Capital One has enjoyed enormous growth—building its headquarters in McLean, Virginia, and creating a company culture and environment that many have regarded as one of the best in the world. In fact, *Fortune* magazine named Capital One to its "100 Best Companies to Work For" list.[7] As Capital One has grown, they have focused not just on their own bottom line but on the bottom line of their customers and raising spending and consumer awareness, launching a budgeting app for consumers, called ENO in 2019. In their drive to change how people relate to their own money and where it is kept, Capital One has launched a "This is Banking Reimagined" campaign and has created banking cafes in partnership with Peet's Coffee, inviting places where people can bank, plan their financial future with a money coach, engage with community, and enjoy a cup of coffee.

But perhaps its most controversial move has been to the cloud. While adapting to a rapidly changing banking market, Capital One has taken advantage of advances in FinTech, core banking, D2C retail customer apps and moved away from legacy systems (in-house developed banking software). They have now begun to operate on the cloud, making their bank more agile, versatile, fast, and infinitely scalable. In doing so, they have faced scrutiny for such a move, and it was called into further question after a hack exposed millions of consumers' data in late July 2019. Though the hack was not caused by the cloud server, but an individual employed at Amazon Web Services, the cloud provider, Capital One is no less dealing with the fallout of a common potential threat to all American businesses. You'll find out here how they dealt with the security breach, how they ensure the integrity and safety of their data, and the ongoing innovation and steps they are taking to mitigate these risks in the future.

Ultimately, you'll learn how two men with a vision and unique approach to data-driven marketing built a new kind of bank. You'll understand the inner workings of the bank and the consumer credit industry, how banking is being reimagined constantly, and just how important our financial institutions are not just to our past and present, but our future as well.

> **You'll learn how two men with a vision and unique approach to data-driven marketing built a new kind of bank.**

"Eighty percent of strategy is figuring out where the world is going and twenty percent is figuring out what you're going to do in response. If you can figure out where the world is going, what you need to do usually becomes obvious. That's why we're always working backwards from end games at Capital One. The whole story of Capital One is about capitalizing on the inexorable evolution of consumer marketing."[1]

—RICHARD FAIRBANK

CHAPTER ONE

THE FOUNDERS' STORY

Nigel Morris and Richard Fairbank

S itting on a stage with a young entrepreneur at Startup Grind in Washington, DC, Nigel Morris is relaxed and settles into the chair.[2] He's been asked to talk to a room full of entrepreneurs, business leaders, and CEO hopefuls about how he and his cofounder, Richard Fairbank, built a new kind of bank, based on data, information-based strategy (IBS), and technology, and why he eventually left Capital One to help fund finance and tech (FinTech) startups. The M.C. introduces Morris as the "Tooth Fairy" of the FinTech industry. *He gives a lot of money away, but no one ever sees him.* The room laughs. They get the joke. However, Morris looks bemused if not a bit confused. Though a private person, he frequently keynotes at industry-leading conferences, including Money2020, LendIt, Finance Disrupted, and the Bernstein Annual Financials Summit. As the founder and CEO of QED Investors, an investment firm located in Alexandria, Virginia, Morris is not shy and is as accessible as one can be for being one of the world's leading venture capitalists. It is his long-time friend and Capital One founder Richard Fairbank, the current CEO of Capital One who enjoys keeping the low profile. Tatiana Stead, a spokeswoman for Capital One, says, "Rich has never been interested in developing a public profile. He has always been singularly focused on the company and his vision for Capital One."[3] That is not to say, Morris isn't "singularly focused." He's just no longer working for Capital One. Outside of public lectures and forums, the two rarely give interviews. So the room is dying to hear just how Morris and Fairbank were able to do what no other banker had done up until 1994—pioneer an IBS that transformed the consumer lending industry and what we all have come to understand to be "modern banking."

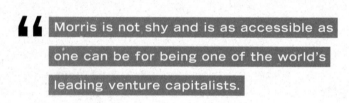

> Morris is not shy and is as accessible as one can be for being one of the world's leading venture capitalists.

What No Other Banker Had Done Up Until 1994

With an unpretentious air and subtle English accent, Morris begins by explaining he was born in the UK and went to eleven different schools while growing up. He does not come from a long line of polished blue bloods or a wealthy banking pedigree, he assures the crowd. His father was in the army, and he spent his childhood moving around quite a lot. His mother was Welsh and spoke it as well. English was her second language. Despite all the moving, he spent his young adulthood like many young English boys playing rugby. He didn't have much of an eye on the future of banking, let alone business in general. In fact, if you had asked him as a teenager what he was going to be when he grew up, traditional banking wouldn't have made the short list. Rather, he was interested in human psychology. Originally, he went to university to become a clinical psychologist, but he came out the program a self-proclaimed "raving empiricist" saying that "if it can't be measured it doesn't exist."

Seduced by data, numbers, and all things that can be proven and measured, Morris attended the London Business School where he graduated with an MBA with distinction and eventually moved onto the Wharton School of Business at the University of Pennsylvania in Philadelphia. When Morris left Wharton, Richard Fairbank hired him for a consultancy position at Strategic Planning Associates (SPA) located in the historic Watergate Building in Washington, DC. It was a unique consultancy for its time and was, what Morris calls, "a data-rich place." Unlike other well-known consultancy firms in the eighties, SPA focused more on business strategy than management. Though fresh-faced and plucked straight from business school, Morris found himself sitting beside Fairbank who was leading strategy for major US financial institutions.

Fairbank's Parents

While Morris is a self-professed raving empiricist, Fairbank was by all means a man steeped in the scientific method himself. By and large, he had little choice in the matter. Fairbank's father, Professor William Fairbank, was a highly regarded and awarded American physicist known for his work on liquid helium and quarks. One of his most famous experiments resulted in the

Gravity Probe B that launched in 2004, which took place some twenty-five years after his death. It was a satellite-based mission that tested two unverified predictions of Einstein's theory of relativity. The elder Fairbank was, by all means, a genius and dreamer, daring to ask questions few others thought to and seeing far into the future where others could not.

Richard's mother, Jane Davenport, was also a successful physicist in her own right. After the outbreak of World War II, both Jane and William were invited to leave graduate school and join the war project to develop shipborne radar at the MIT Radiation Laboratory. Today, she is renowned as a pioneer for women in physics and only the second female graduate student in physics at the University of Washington and the second woman scientist employed at the MIT Radiation Laboratory. Following the war, she retired from physics to raise her family. Despite all her professional accomplishments and achievements, till the end she maintained that her "sons were her greatest accomplishment."[4]

Richard grew up with two brothers, in a loving, active, and cerebral home, near Stanford University, where his father served as a professor. It was there he watched firsthand the power of forming experiments and collecting data. More importantly, it's where he learned to dare to ask questions others didn't think to ask. Fairbank's father was a deeply thoughtful and inquisitive man. In Dr. Fairbank's *New York Times* obituary, Francis Everitt, one of Dr. Fairbank's colleagues at Stanford, said that Dr. Fairbank devoted much of his career to "doing experiments nobody believed could be done."[5]

Every bit as analytical and scientific-thinking, Richard Fairbank had no intention of following in his father's footsteps. Though he attended Stanford University, he was not, in his own words a "typical student." He had enjoyed working with children and was recruited to work as a manager for a recreation agency. While working with children, he also became passionate about his studies in economics. Eventually, he went back to school and earned his MBA from Stanford University, graduating the first in his class. After graduation he went into consulting. By the time Fairbank hired Morris at SPA in Washington, DC, Fairbank's father's experiential mind and willingness to do what others thought can't be done began to reveal itself even more in his own. *Like father, like son.* After all, Fairbank was an experiential scientist at heart. He thought of ideas and hypotheses, created experiments, tested them, evaluated the data, and based his conclusions on the results.

To this day, as the CEO and Chairman of Capital One, he is every bit the scientist—and deliberate strategist—who isn't afraid to do what others won't or say can't be done. Known as a bit of a "contrarian" by those he has worked with, he is comfortable pushing people out of their comfort zones and is always willing to try new things. "He likes to be zigging when the world is zagging," said Gary Perlin, who retired in 2014 as chief financial officer. "He likes to be a contrarian because that's where he sees the greatest opportunities. And he's willing to change his mind."[6] Especially when the data calls for it. Tom Brown, CEO of hedge fund Second Curve Capital, an adviser and investor in Capital One when it went public says, "They had a completely different way of doing business, a testing and learning approach that was completely innovative. Rich [Fairbank] is so nontraditionally thoughtful. He's able to see into the future of where he needs to be and work backward, even when no one else agrees."[7]

> " To this day, as the CEO and Chairman of Capital One, he is every bit the scientist—and deliberate strategist—who isn't afraid to do what others won't or say can't be done.

From the beginning, Fairbank was willing to do things in a way no one else had done before. In a 1996 annual report he wrote, "Capital One began with a strategic vision: clear, dynamic, inexorable. We saw that the technology and information revolution had transformed the credit card business into an information business. One that is extraordinarily data-rich, allowing the capture of information on every customer interaction and transaction. With this information, we can conduct scientific tests; build actuarially based models of consumer behavior; and tailor products, pricing, credit lines, and account management to meet the individual needs and wants of each customer. By exploiting this insight, we have transformed the one-size-fits-all credit card industry and created one of the fastest-growing companies in America. Because our strategy is information-based, not product-based, we are in an excellent position to ride the macro trend of the information revolution and apply our strategy to other industries as they too are reshaped by information."[8]

This revolutionary idea to use IBS when creating products and services became the foundation on which Fairbank built the company.

The Big Idea

One could argue both Morris and Fairbank are wired to test and look for results, but it also came out of sheer necessity early in their careers. While working at SPA, Fairbank became increasingly interested in how information and technology were changing the world of consumer marketing. They were also keenly aware of the need for smart problem-solving to optimize performance at companies. As a consultant, Fairbank began to see "patterns across different industries" and began to generate a few deeply held beliefs that would ultimately shape his thinking. The first belief was that the industry structure was the key determining factor in the success of a company. The second belief was as he says, "when the world changes, often the last people to know are the ones most deeply involved in the old way."[9]

The advantage he had as a consultant with an outsider's perspective was what he also credits to the success of Capital One. "The story of Capital One is the power of an objective ignorant view of the world from someone who really didn't know anything about the credit card business," Fairbank explains.[10] Neither young man had experience as bank executives themselves, and suddenly they found themselves sitting before Big Bank execs and consulting them. They had to rely on asking probing questions, listening, and observing before jumping to conclusions.

In some ways not having worked inside banks had its advantages as well. Rather than coming from a place of expertise or "this is how it's always been done" Fairbank and Morris could look at the issues banks were facing with a completely new and outside perspective. "I think that sometimes when the world is ripe for change, the less you know, the less you have to separate conventional wisdom from real wisdom,"[11] Fairbank adds. It would also mean he would have to rely on data—not anecdotes—to draw conclusions and make strategic suggestions.

> **"** The story of Capital One is the power of an objective ignorant view of the world from someone who really didn't know anything about the credit card business."

The two men spent a lot of time together and got to know each other, and quickly realized they were both passionate about the same thing. They loved working together to tackle big questions and issues the Big Banks in New York were facing. Their primary job was looking at the entire bank conglomerate and figuring out where the biggest returns on investment were. Explaining how they did that to the crowd of entrepreneurs before him, Morris explains, "You busted a bank up into its constituent parts and divided up the amount of equity and you figured out where the bank was making a great amount of money."

It was there in that data that Morris says the seeds were being planted in Fairbank's mind for a new way to think about banking. Morris recalls, "We found time after time there was this business called *the credit card business*. It was growing at twenty and thirty percent a year. And, it was making thirty to forty percent on equity. And candidly, it wasn't being managed by the superstar of the bank. The superstars were working on investment banking."

Fairbank had several additional observations he shared in an interview with Stanford University business students: "First, the fact that everyone had the same price (same APR and annual fees) for credit cards in a risk-based business was strange. It was clear that credit cards would be a very profitable business if people actually paid you back. Underlying the strong probability in the business was a massively steep gradient of customer profitability. And, if you could de-average that underlying profitability gradient (because you could lose your shirt when people don't pay you back), you could build a profitable business. Secondly, credit cards were a profoundly rich information business because, with the information revolution, there was a huge amount of information that could be acquired about the customers externally. Finally, the industry lends itself to massive scientific testing because it has millions of customers and a very flexible product where the terms and nature of the product can be individualized and the channel of marketing was direct marketing where literally a unique offer could be made to every single customer."[12]

Intrigued by these findings, it was clear to Fairbank what strategic direction banks should be taking. He recruited Morris to help launch the IBS concept and find a sponsor. Fairbank planned to pitch banks on the concept of using IBS to build a card portfolio, tailoring each product to a market niche. Fairbank and Morris then met with twenty to twenty-five heads of credit card divisions or CEOs. The men pitched a combination of "scientific testing of product and pricing features and the uses of behavioral and actuarial principles in the data mining of consumers," as well as innovative ideas regarding credit scoring, underwriting, and collections.

Fairbank was met with a less than enthusiastic reply from all the banks he visited. He recalls, "Every issuer had the same price for everybody. That's a ridiculous notion. It's as if the auto insurance industry had the same price for 16-year-olds as they had for forty-six-year-olds."[13] Selling the idea to the banks was easier said than done.

"We sold zero," Morris recalls the time he and Fairbank traveled the country talking to banks and trying to convince them of this service. "They would listen to us and then say it can't be done." Morris says the two men grew accustomed to hearing the oft-spoken reply, "You're just two business school graduates and strategy consultants." *What could they possibly know about banking or running a financial institution?* In fact, every single bank executive turned Fairbank and his idea down, some more graciously than others. One CEO even threatened to "throw Fairbank out of the window if he ever again recommended a business with charge-off rates over one percent."[14] Fairbank recalls over half of the banks citing the reason for the decline was that they were already using IBS (simply because they used computers), while other said they couldn't possibly implement such a plan. Fairbank adds, "Some said it would cause too much internal difficulty, that they would have to realign the firm."[15] Fairbank is quick to add that this is an entirely "correct assessment" because he explains, "creating a culture of constantly challenging ideas and introducing the complexity of mass customization can mean profound changes to an organization."[16]

" Morris says the two men grew accustomed to hearing the oft-spoken reply, "You're just two business school graduates and strategy consultants." *What could they possibly know about banking or running a financial institution?*

Looking at the Data

The two men weren't discouraged though. In their minds this was a "fantastic" business opportunity. Morris remembers when they were beginning to tease out the details of a new venture and knew that if they were to do something it would have to be done differently than how banks were doing it then. "And boy were there opportunities to do it differently," Morris says. The two worked through just how they would do things differently and were sure of their proposal. They asked themselves, "What if we gave everybody the same product at the same price, and we started to discriminate based just on underlying risk for example?" In other words, instead of shutting someone out because they never had a credit card before, or because their birthdate didn't match their social security card (which was the case for Morris, who was not born in the US and that is the case for many immigrants or naturalized citizens), they could use data. "Instead, we can *actuarially* prevent risk, like they do in car insurance." For example, they could run extensive tests—tens of thousands of tests, in fact.[17]

In an interview with Nanette Byrnes from Bloomberg, Fairbank and Morris disclosed just what those tests reveal, "Someone who spends 45 minutes online researching a car purchase, for instance, is a good credit risk for the company's auto lending arm. But someone who calls up to apply for a credit card is riskier than someone who responds to a solicitation." Byrnes acknowledges in the article that "Testing has been derided by critics as gimmicky, but it proved its value during the recession as Capital One's bad-loan and charge-off rates remained in check, while other lenders saw them balloon."[18] The reason for this, according to Morris, is in the numbers. They could do what others couldn't because they were working a large pool of consumers and they were paying close attention to what their behavior was telling them. "At the time, the credit card game in the late eighties was one-size-fits-all. One price for everyone. However only half of Americans had credit cards, and the other half all got the same product," Morris adds.

That's where data came in, Morris contends. "If we could look at the data, we could really understand actuarial risk." In other words, could a consumer be counted on to pay back what he or she owed? They also wanted to understand the unique needs of the consumer. "Some want an annual fee for a lower APR, others want points. Some people want a picture of the dog on the plastic card."

For Morris and Fairbank, the credit card industry was a "giant laboratory, in which we could do two things: unleash infinite test and learn capabilities to figure out what products we could offer to the right person at the right price and do that with actuarial precision, and at the same time use the net present value (NPV) as the currency to compare ideas so you could fully optimize the whole laboratory." For Fairbank the vision was even more simple: "The vision was to smash the price of credit," he says.[19] It was also simple in another way: The data would reveal all. It would show what the customer wanted and needed, and it would help Fairbank and Morris then create products that matched those needs.

To Morris and Fairbank, the idea seemed like a slam dunk. They saw the data, the profit margins, the untapped opportunity. All they needed to do was sell the idea to the Big Banks. However, as all business leaders, sales people, and entrepreneurs know, it only takes one fish to bite. After a year of flying all over the country, in 1988, Signet Bank in Richmond, Virginia, was game. There was only one stipulation. Signet wanted Morris and Fairbank to be *all in*. The two men had to leave the cushy consultancy world behind and begin working for Signet full-time in their Richmond offices. Fairbank and Morris agreed to accept the job offers, however, they too had a few stipulations. They wanted to have control not only of the credit card division's strategy, marketing, and credit functions, but also the information technology functions (which resided in corporate). Fairbank also negotiated a new form of compensation—he and certain executives would receive significant shares of the net present value (NPV) of any new accounts generated. Signet agreed and Fairbank and Morris joined Signet in October 1989.[20]

But What Did Others Say?
Dealing with Naysayers

When Fairbank and Morris went back to their colleagues at SPA to tell them about Signet's job offer, they were met with less than enthusiastic replies. A senior partner at SPA was downright confused. Fairbank recalls the man saying to him, "How can you do this? You're joining Cigna!?" Fairbank had to clarify and explain he wasn't leaving the consulting firm for an insurance provider. "No, no. I said, Signet," Fairbank explained. The partner then wondered, "What's that? Are you gonna run the place?" And Fairbank countered, "No, no. In credit cards, I'm just going to . . ." And the partner cut him off and asked incredulously, "Run the credit card division?"

No one could see what Fairbank and Morris could see— mainly the opportunity. To everyone on the outside it looked like a step down for the two men.

But it just wasn't their own colleagues who were naysayers. The men met a different kind of resistance in Signet as well. As mentioned earlier, Fairbank and Morris had some conditions on which they would accept the offer to work for Signet, and one of them was that the men had complete control of the credit card division's strategy, marketing, and information technology (IT) functions. Signet couldn't understand the demands. A Signet executive said to Fairbank, "That's funny, Rich, I didn't know you're an expert on systems." And Fairbank responded, "No, and neither is Nigel. Other than a few classes in business school, we don't know all that much about technology. But we know exactly what we want out of technology, and we believe technology is going to be the central nervous system of our information-based strategy. We need to have the technology folks sitting side by side with analysts and marketing folks, all co-developing strategies and systems, and that's why we need them all reporting to me."[21]

> **Other than a few classes in business school, we don't know all that much about technology. But we know exactly what we want out of technology, and we believe technology is going to be the central nervous system of our information-based strategy."**

The concepts of DevOps and "breaking down silos and departments" was still decades away from the mainstream. Most companies and banks worked in a classic eighties *Dirty Dancing*-style kind of way. Who can forget Patrick Swayze's character Johnny Castle warning Baby, "This is my dance space, this is your dance space. I don't go into yours. You don't go into mine." Everyone had to stick to their own turf. But, Fairbank and Morris knew that those days were—like Baby and Johnny's summer fling at Kellerman's—*over*.

Near-Death Experiences and Lessons Learned

As always when new leadership comes on board there is bound to be resistance within the ranks, especially from those who are comfortable with the way things have always been done in their territory. Since Fairbank and Morris didn't have authority to change the organization and structure of Signet's non-credit card businesses, they had to, as Fairbank said, "work from within and laterally to try to make things happen." One of their main oppositions was a man named Dan Oelrich, who was renowned within the industry for his "expertise in judgmental credit policy." Basically a "judgmental credit policy" was one in which credit analysts used their "specialized training and experience" (though that wasn't really defined) to assess an applicant's records before reaching what they called an "informed" though clearly unscientific decision.

In some cases, one could argue it worked. Under Oelrich's leadership Signet's credit division had one of the lowest charge-off rates in history. However, Fairbank and Morris argued that this policy wasn't sustainable. "Relying on your tummy to make decisions," Fairbank contended wasn't scalable. Nor could judgmental credit policies, he argued, "fully exploit information because credit analysts' insights and experiences were not easily transferable to other analysts."[22] In order to change the policy they had to run some initial tests. But, their first test was nothing short of disastrous. Signet's charge off rate rose from 2 percent, one of the industry's best, to more than 6 percent, among the industry's worst.[23]

"It was a terrifying situation," Morris admits. "We tragically got the numbers wrong and how costly it was." The two young men were feeling the heat, and often felt stressed. While in the car together on their commutes to and from Richmond from their homes in the DC area, they would talk and wonder aloud each day, "I wonder if this is the day we'll be fired." Nothing was working out, Morris recalls, and he remembers one time his friend encouraging him, "Nigel, it's always darkest before the dawn." And according to Morris, "It was pretty dark." Fairbank recalls the same time period with similar gravity: "It took four years of near-death experiences to have our first success."[24] In fact, Fairbank believed it was a "matter of days or weeks or, at most, months before our venture would be shut down."[25]

As if perfectly timed, however, the leaders of the bank weren't entirely concerned with the slow progress of the credit card division. The bank was dealing with another crisis of their own. Their real estate division was having serious issues, and all the efforts and focus of the company was there. Though a difficult time for the bank, it freed Morris and Fairbank up to retool, rework, troubleshoot, improve their processes, hire better talent who could better manage and lead the customer service, all the while refining their offerings using the data they were collecting on their customers.

Their main goal in the beginning was to find everyone paying 19.8 percent and APR, with competitors (and who were also actuarially low risk) and then reach them by direct mail. Their essential message was: "Don't pay 19.8 percent. With us you can pay 9.9 percent." They would offer a considerably lower rate to proven payers, essentially rewarding good behavior. All the customer had to do was sign a check that came to them in the mail and do a balance transfer. At the time, most consumers were unaware of just how much they were paying and everyone was basically paying the same amount.

While lowering interest and offering balance transfers is seen as a noble enterprise for those in the banking world, some financial experts still warn people like you and me against taking out any kind of credit, let alone balance transfers. Popular for his down-home wisdom about money, bestselling author and radio host Dave Ramsey, argues you can't borrow your way out of debt and often warns against balance transfers or personal loans. He believes the only one making any money on these ventures is the banks. Low interest balance transfers only work if you pay off the amount you transferred in a very quick time period, because once the promotional time ends (usually six months to a year) with the low balances, the interest rate increases. Some people get into trouble with balance transfers because they don't realize the impact it can have on their credit score. Each balance transfer application usually takes 10 points off your score. So if you're looking to get a car loan or a buy a house within a year of a balance transfer, you may want to think twice. Another way customers can get into trouble with balance transfers is that they enjoy the lower minimum payments a bit too much, and don't feel the incentive to pay off their card with the lower interest quickly enough. Over time this can add up. Still another way borrowers can get into trouble with a balance transfer is if they now have more available credit on their other card and they don't have enough self-discipline to not charge on that card, they could find themselves in even more debt.

While yes, it's ideal not use credit cards, Fairbank and Morris were working within the system that was already profiting enormously from people's lack of knowledge of how credit worked and they sought to make it better—and forcing other banks to as well. By lowering their interest rates to 9.9 percent they opened the floodgates for banks to do the same.

The second part of their idea was changing the concept of *who* was credit worthy. Only half of Americans had access to credit cards. "It was the age-old, thin-file problem," Morris asserts. They didn't have credit, so they couldn't get credit. "We wanted to democratize it," Morris argues. "Having access to plastic was necessary to run people's lives." Renting cars, staying in hotels, establishing a credit history to buy a home—all of this was out of reach for many previously thought "ineligible" consumers. Ethan Cohen-Cole, a PhD in economics from University of Wisconsin and author of *Credit Card Redlining*, conducted a study on socio-economic and racial discrimination in the credit card industry and argues, "Credit cards are the first step on the financial ladder."[26] Morris and Fairbank agreed and wanted to level the playing field. To do so they wanted to use data to help, rather than harm using outdated and discriminatory practices. Ultimately, they wanted to see what the consumer wanted and needed and respond to those needs.

It Takes Discipline

Just as they were disciplined in their approach in gathering research and data as consultants, they were equally as disciplined when running the credit card agency. They piloted, measured results, and responded to those results. They formed hypotheses, created models, tested those models on small testing groups and waited for the results. "We made sure we had the economics nailed down and we knew the answers before we rolled it out," Morris recalls. This methodical and disciplined approach proved to be a winning recipe for success. They tested hundreds of approaches to new products. Thanks to what Fairbank calls the "explosively successful" national roll out of the 9.9 percent low-introductory rate, they enjoyed massive gains. Within three years, Signet's credit card business grew to approximately five million customers and $7 billion in managed loans.[27] The business went from near death to hiring a 100-person team in a week to execute the successful balance transfer product and drive the growth of Signet's business.

> **Within three years, Signet's credit card business grew to approximately five million customers and $7 billion in managed loans. The business went from near death to hiring a 100-person team in a week to execute the successful balance transfer product and drive the growth of Signet's business.**

The credit card division grew exponentially under Morris's and Fairbank's leadership. In fact, the credit cards division's revenues and products began to overtake the rest of the bank. So much so, when the securities analysts came to review Signet's books, they said there was a huge opportunity for shareholders. If the credit division spun off, investors would receive what Morris called a "Conglomerate discount, where two plus two equals five." Those in charge of the bank agreed that it was the right thing to do for the shareholders and determined it was time to spin off the credit card division into an IPO in 1994.

Family Comes First

Morris admits it was great opportunity, though terrifying. At just forty-four years old, Richard Fairbank, would be the CEO, and Nigel Morris, thirty-six, would be the COO and president of their own bank. When Fairbank told his wife and college sweetheart, Chris, about the offer, she cried. It was not out of joy or excitement. Rather, she was deeply concerned. Fairbank recalls her saying, "I am afraid that in the context of a public company, they are going to change who you are."[28] Chris Fairbank has always been moral and ethical sounding board for Fairbank. She is nothing if not frank. When Fairbank was in graduate school she said to him, "you grossed me out" when she saw him getting swept up in what his peers were doing and what they were excited about—working for prestigious companies and striving for high salaries. She grounded him. Besides the inherent danger of being "changed" there was a more immediate concern for Chris as well: time. They were a young family.

The entire time Fairbank was working as a consultant and Signet he made family a priority. Fairbank promised his wife he would spend an average of two and half hours a night with their children. Despite his travel schedule—sometimes flying up to New York and back in the same day as a consultant and commuting back and forth between DC and Richmond while at Signet—Fairbank had promised he would be at home each night. Since he had such long days, the two came up with an unlikely strategy that most parent coaches and sleep experts today would be horrified by: His young children would stay up until midnight, sleep in the morning, and attend preschool later in the afternoon. Fairbank, despite all the obstacles, was willing to take the risk and doubled down on his parental responsibilities, vowing to his wife if he "changed" or he couldn't see the kids, he would quit "immediately."[29]

The Unique Strategy
That Drove Their Early Success:
Information-Based Strategy (IBS)

The early years in Signet were formative ones. It was there the two men developed and honed their now proprietary IBS. Using advanced information technology and sophisticated quantitative analysis, they mined vast amounts of data they collected on millions of actual and prospective customers. Within two years of going public with Capital One, they had exceeded their own expectations, in large part because of their IBS. In a 1996 Annual Report, Fairbank explained the strategy and methodology in detail, writing, "We use the data and scientific methodology to test many product ideas on a small scale, allowing us to separate winners from losers before we make major commitments to marketing. By the time we invest in a large-scale product launch, we already know we can count on superior economic returns. The information-based strategy also gives us the ability to customize our offerings in order to get the right product to the right customer at the right time and at the right price. We now have more than 3,000 products, pricing and feature combinations tailored to the individual needs and wants of our customers. By designing and pricing products to fit each customer's financial circumstances, we have been able to add almost seven million customers in the last four years. Customization also enables us to offer our products at highly competitive rates while simultaneously generating favorable returns for Capital One."[30]

It wasn't just IBS that they developed at Signet. It was the mindset around innovation and technology as well. Fairbank writes, "We believe that every business or product idea has a limited shelf life."[31] Knowing this, they built everything with the end in mind—planning for the inevitable end of a product's life cycle. The hope was, Fairbank adds, "to stay ahead of the downtrend by introducing a steady stream of product innovations." One such example he provides is how initially they were the first bank in the nation to offer balance transfer products nationwide. Like most successful product innovations, it drew a crowd of competitors and, over time, became less profitable. However, Fairbank anticipated this development well in advance and had scaled up the investment into what he deemed "a new, second generation of products even while the balance transfer product was still enjoying strong growth."[32] These second generation products, which capitalized on their ability to customize offerings for a wide range of specialty segments included secured cards, college student cards, affinity cards, and a variety of cards for underserved markets.

These new products, coupled with introductory rates, contributed to a dramatic surge in revenue early on. By 1996, Capital One's total revenue (managed net interest income plus non-interest income) grew 63 percent to $1.5 billion from $906 million in 1995.

Fairbank credited the information-based strategy in giving them the ability to make "opportunistic moves even with mature products" and to mitigate risk. Fairbank explains, "Consumer credit is a cyclical business and, unlike many industry observers, we believe that the problems of the current cycle have yet to peak. Our information-based strategy gives us the data and the tools to manage risk effectively. We use sophisticated models to analyze risk, and we base our decisions on highly conservative forecasts. To minimize total credit exposure . . . products are also priced and structured to provide appropriate risk coverage at the individual customer level. The combination of our strategy and our conservatism was critical to our record performance in a difficult year for the credit card business."[33]

Also important to Capital One's early strong growth was their ability to harness the power of cutting-edge information technology and use it to create a highly flexible operating infrastructure. This infrastructure allowed them to bring new ideas to market much more quickly than their competition. In fact, their success in integrating information technology into every aspect of their business earned Capital One the Gartner Group's 1996 Excellence in Technology Award given annually *to only one* company in the United States. The award is one of the most prestigious in its field. Past winners include UPS, American Airlines, and Federal Express.[34]

" Capital One earned the Gartner Group's 1996 Excellence in Technology Award given annually *to only one* company in the United States.

As the information revolution increasingly transformed other consumer products and services, Fairbank doubled down on his belief that strategy and technology would enable them to seize a competitive advantage in the marketplace.

Establishing Core Value and Principles from the Outset

Capital One's sustained success, Fairbank contends, is the product of a set of principles they have embraced since bringing the information-based strategy (IBS) to Signet in 1988. These principles, the essence of Capital One, combined strategic insights and management values, which they refined through years of consulting and entrepreneurship and tailored to the unique requirements of their IBS. These principles were not just something they talked about; they were and are a way of life at Capital One. One employee, asking not to be named, says: "It's absolutely true. I wouldn't be here if they weren't true. The leaders walk the walk." The principles she is talking about are woven into the fabric of the company, and have been a part of it since day one. Fairbank admits, it wasn't easy to establish these principles, stating, "Implementing them has required rebuilding the Company from the ground up and challenging many of the core assumptions upon which large companies are typically built."[35]

Besides the IBS and utilizing technology, one of their core principles was recruiting as well. Fairbank writes, "Recruiting is Capital One's most important business. We don't just say it, we live it." The complexity of their strategy and unending innovation demanded world-class talent—what Fairbank calls, "intellectual and executional superstars." Just as they used IBS to enhance credit offerings, they used them to find the best candidates and measure their performance through comprehensive tests and interviews. Anyone who works there or who has been through the rigorous process knows that the standards are extraordinarily high. Fairbank writes, "Our senior management is extensively involved throughout the recruiting process. After hiring the very best of the best, we work hard to develop them through training programs, exposure to management, coaching, job rotation and early opportunities for unusually broad responsibility. We view our career development efforts as critical in building the competencies required by Capital One's information-based strategy. Our information-based strategy begins with hiring exceptional talent—talent that is eager to seize challenges, to take ownership as soon as problems arise, and to make solutions happen."[36]

But they don't stop there. Fairbank adds, "Knowing that our associates need an environment which supports peak performance, we have created and nurtured a culture of entrepreneurship, which we believe is one of the most distinctive assets of Capital One. We encourage our associates to think and act like owners. And we challenge our managers to see themselves not as bosses but as coaches dedicated to empowering every player by providing direction, leading by example, setting extraordinary standards, and keeping our very fast track clear of the usual bureaucratic barriers to high performance."[37] Capital One has spread the spirit of ownership throughout the company by making all associates eligible for their employee stock ownership program, as well as their 401(K) plan and stock options.

A key virtue that Capital One looks for in its staff is something they believe in completely for the company as well—or what they call "near infinite flexibility." Recognizing the transitory and ever-evolving nature of its business, the leaders know many of their business opportunities are short-lived. "We have to move fast to exploit them and move on when they fade. We strive to see the world through the eyes of our customers, not through our organizational structures," Fairbank writes. "Inter-departmental teamwork is a way of life at Capital One, with players constantly crossing boundaries, changing jobs and forming new teams to meet evolving needs inside the Company and in the marketplace."[38]

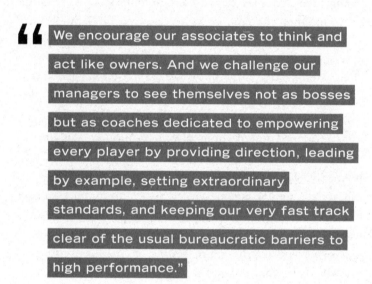

> We encourage our associates to think and act like owners. And we challenge our managers to see themselves not as bosses but as coaches dedicated to empowering every player by providing direction, leading by example, setting extraordinary standards, and keeping our very fast track clear of the usual bureaucratic barriers to high performance."

The Value of Communication

This means at the heart of what Fairbank calls "near-infinite flexibility" resides another essential principle and value at the core of Capital One: communication. Honest, forthright, direct, yet, gracious communication from "top-down, bottom-up and across departments" is nonstop to ensure that all employees act on complete, up-to-the-minute information. "With our integrated systems and people, Capital One is endlessly flexible, able to reshape itself again and again to make the most of our opportunities," Fairbank says.[39]

While Capital One's strategy is one of aggressive growth through innovation, it is anchored in what Fairbank calls "a culture of conservatism." That is not to say the political conservatism, which can conjure all sorts of allusions or biases or conclusions. Rather he means it in the truest sense of the word: *Cautious. Pragmatic. Measured.* Fairbank adds, "Our innovation is pragmatic, tied to a rigorous discipline of testing, which lets us know in advance which ideas are likely to succeed in the marketplace. New products are not rolled out unless they demonstrate an ability to deliver superior returns. We forecast the inevitable decline of existing opportunities, plan for the obsolescence of our products, and challenge the organization to find new sources of growth. While our management of credit risk employs highly sophisticated statistical models, extensive testing and monitoring, and constant recalibration of models as markets move, we understand that credit risk is partly driven by external factors beyond our control. So we fortify our position with large financial buffers, one of the industry's lowest average credit limits, stringent credit underwriting and flexible products—all designed to help us weather adverse credit developments."[40]

Building a Brand and Bank from Scratch

After establishing their core values and principles, one of the first things the men had to do was differentiate themselves from the other players in the market. The men knew their company's competitive advantage was their IBS, unlike American Express

whose competitive advantage was brand, Citibank's was econo-
mies of scale, or MBNA's, with its many links to affinity groups.[41]
But, IBS was not a name or a way to reach their market. They
had to create trustworthiness and awareness—and to do so they
needed a name. Something totally different than Signet.

They narrowed the field down two options—Global One
and Capital One. They chose Capital One—an obvious nod to
money and because they were in the capital city, Washington,
DC, and had no plans to move the bank. But mostly because
someone had already claimed Global One.

> **They chose Capital One—an obvious nod to money and because they were in the capital city, Washington, DC, and had no plans to move the bank.**

Largely unheard of, and now operating without the Signet
brand, Capital One had to figure out a way to gain the trust of
the consumer. They decided to use the Visa/MasterCard brand
names on their cards. But, they knew that they couldn't rely on
the Visa/MasterCard brand alone forever. If they wanted to
play in the big leagues and compete with other major banks,
they had to invest in marketing and branding. "We figured it
would cost between $100 and $150 million a year," Morris says.

It was a shocking sum for a fledgling company, but they
knew with something as sensitive as credit, they had to build a
trustworthy brand. The problem was they had trained everyone
in their company to believe that you couldn't spend money on
anything or take a risk unless you absolutely could prove that it

would net positive results. Anyone working in branding and marketing or any creative venture knows that *absolutely* knowing if a brand message or commercial will work is nearly impossible to predict. Morris recalls hearing people in the company saying, "Nigel and Rich are off the reservation." Morris agrees they were indeed going off script but admits, "We had to try."

In 2000, Morris and Fairbank pulled a branding team together and worked with a top New York ad agency where Keith Goldberg was one of the copywriters assigned. Morris and Fairbank were intentional about what they wanted. They told Goldberg and the branding team they wanted to "shock people into really taking control of their own financials. The idea was to attack the inertia around carrying plastic around and to get people to really think about where their money was going."

Goldberg claims it was the "most challenging assignment" of his career. Tasked with helping the upstart credit card take on JP Morgan, Chase, Citi, BNY, Mellon, and become a major financial services player was not for the faint of heart. Goldberg adds, "We wanted to make the card issuer actually add value and provoke doubt in consumers' minds regarding the value of their legacy card choices. That's how 'What's in your wallet?' was born. When I wrote that tagline, I had no idea it would blow up like it has."[42]

"What's in your wallet?" is considered one of world's most iconic tag lines and was installed on New York's Advertising Walk of Fame in 2011 along with others like Wendy's eighties' iconic "Where's the Beef?"[43] With that tagline they found, what Morris called, "velocity" with the brand. "It got us over Visa and MasterCard, and it enabled us to open up to mortgages, car loans, etc," Morris says.

This all sounds like it was smooth sailing in the beginning. But, Morris says, it looked a lot easier than it was. "At the time we were at the edge of what we could do." Morris and Fairbank were well aware of what they were up against, namely legacy banks with a proven track record dating back literally hundreds of years. Capital One was a disrupter. They were David taking on Goliath. They were also dealing with a largely unaware consumer market who had not ever thought to question what the big banks were doing for centuries. Finally, there weren't really a traditional or legacy bank at all. Morris argues, "Capital One was essentially a technology company selling credit cards. We took a disciplined test-and-learn approach and data analytics further than anyone. And to this day, very few banks have pulled the same off."

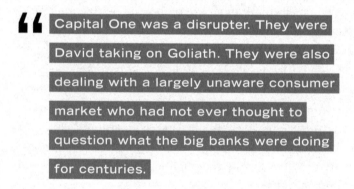

> Capital One was a disrupter. They were David taking on Goliath. They were also dealing with a largely unaware consumer market who had not ever thought to question what the big banks were doing for centuries.

This, Morris contends, is largely cultural. Legacy banks are slow to change and are steeped in tradition. In addition, the regulatory pressures are so austere it's difficult to create what he calls a startup-like "ecosystem where flourishing ideas can happen." One of the key advantages to being what he deemed "a technology company that sells credit cards" was they could create a startup-like culture and were able to create entrepreneurial incentives in a big company.

While building the company they took what they learned as consultants and then managing a customer service and credit card division at Signet and applied it to their hiring. From the beginning they focused on talent. "The difference between someone who is really good and someone who is phenomenal is massive," Morris contends.

With a focus on disrupting the industry, informing consumers, hiring the best of the best, and creating startup-like culture that could be sustained in a big company, Morris and Fairbank set out to build a world-class consumer-lending company and bank. What they ended up doing exceeded not just their own expectations, but the entire financial world's, and pushed other banks to compete as well, thus changing the playing field for consumers everywhere.

> **Morris and Fairbank set out to build a world-class consumer-lending company and bank. What they ended up doing exceeded not just their own expectations, but the entire financial world's.**

The Founders Now

In 2004, Morris left Capital One at the top of his game. According to his own bio, he is tremendously proud of his ten-year tenure, while not taking entire credit for its success, he does report that "Capital One's net income after taxes (NIAT) grew at a compound annual rate of more than 32 percent. Over this same decade, earnings per share growth and return on equity both exceeded 20 percent per year, a financial performance achieved by only a handful of American companies. Upon leaving Capital One in 2004, the company's 15,000 employees across the United States, Canada, and the United Kingdom managed over $80 billion of loans for 50 million customers. Generating over $1.5 billion in earnings, Capital One had successfully transitioned from an emerging startup to an established public company valued at over $20 billion" by the time Morris left.[44]

Though enjoying monumental success, Morris decided running an international corporation wasn't for him. Unlike his friend Fairbank, Morris wasn't suited for corporate life. He was growing restless and wanted to build things and help others start their own companies—especially young entrepreneurs and startups. After taking a year's sabbatical in the UK to think about his next steps, he returned to the US and cofounded and became the managing partner for QED Investors, a FinTech venture capital platform focused on disruptive, high-growth financial services companies.

According to their website, QED has made numerous investments, including Credit Karma, Nubank, Avant, SoFi, Klarna, GreenSky, and AvidXchange. Today Morris is the chairman of ClearScore and Mission Lane and serves on the boards of Red Ventures, AvidXchange, MediaMath, Prosper, and Zopa. He also serves on Nubank's Board, the board of ideas42, and Scotia's Digital Advisory Council, and he works in an advisory capacity with General Atlantic and Oliver Wyman. Morris previously worked on the boards of Capital One, The Economist, Brookings, National Geographic, Klarna, Braintree, TransUnion, and London Business School. In 2019, he was listed by CB Insights as one of the Top 100 Venture Capitalists. He still lives in Virginia with this wife. He has four children and two grandchildren. He spends his days now looking for the next big thing, but lets the data make the decisions for him.

Fairbank, however, never had to call in the promise he had made to his wife. Corporate life didn't change him. He even had time to coach soccer, basketball, and hockey—for all eight of his children. He never had to quit Capital One. It didn't change him—at least as he says "between the ears" or in the "heart"—where it mattered.[45] A billionaire now, one would never know it by how unassuming and low key he is. An avid hockey player, he plays in an amateur league in the evenings. In fact, in addition to running one of the top ten banks in the US, he co-owns a suburban Virginia hockey rink—where a little team known as the Washington Capitals practice. (The arena the Washington Capitals play in is named Capital One Arena.)

Though the two founders ultimately took different paths after starting Capital One, they are still bonded by the path that got them there—mainly how they looked beyond the way things had always been and had an eye on the future, by understanding consumers' needs, leveraging their own experience to recognize opportunities, taking risks, and, like Dr. William Fairbank, having a willingness to do what others wouldn't do or even thought possible.

"What's in your wallet?"

—CAPITAL ONE

CHAPTER TWO

RAPID EXPANSION AND MARKET DOMINATION

t's a cold, winter's afternoon. A husband exits his car and greets his wife who is outside putting up holiday decorations. "Ho-ho-ho! Happy holidays!" he says, carrying several bags filled with presents through the snow. "I hope you didn't put all those on the credit card," his wife says with a look of concern. Meanwhile a large group of Visigoths are encroaching and on the attack—slaying unsuspecting snowmen and plastic Santas as they charge toward the wary couple. "Do you know what those interest charges are going to do to us?" the wife says, looking over her husband's shoulder at the impending attack. "Don't worry! I used our new Capital One card!" her husband assures her. The Visigoths hear this, drop their weapons, and look at one another in dismay and exasperation. The wife smiles in relief. The Visigoths rally, raise their shields, axes, and swords and shout: "To the neighbors!" as they run next door to raid another family. A voiceover says, "Don't get raided this holiday season. Get a new Capital One card and all your purchases are interest free until May 2001." The wife then looks at her neighbor's house that is being plundered by the Visigoths and says to her husband, "We've got to tell Steve and Laura about Capital One." The voiceover returns: "Capital One." And then asks, "What's in Your Wallet?"[1]

The message in the commercial is clear: *Credit card companies up until Capital One were operating in the Dark Ages.* They were bullies. They were raiding unsuspecting families. They were careless—wiping out anyone and anything in their wake. However, Capital One was a new kind of credit card. The commercial wanted to assure viewers: It cared about families, it cared about interest rates. It wanted to inform people about what was really going on inside their proverbial and physical wallets. The line the wife speaks, "Do you know what those interest charges are going to do to us?" was a calculated statement. At the time, most people with credit cards had little idea of the damage these large interest rates were doing to their financial lives. Capital One was taking a new approach—don't just *sell* to the consumer, *educate* them. This of course, wasn't an accident. This was an intentional approach and strategy from the beginning—and it came out of the data.

In the early years of Capital One, hundreds of millions of dollars were spent on research. Capital One wanted to know what consumers were using, why they were using certain cards, what they wanted, and how much of their decision making was based on facts and information. Capital One was playing the long game. Instead of coming out of the gate hard and strong, they did their research and they focused on branding and marketing to establish trust with a largely unaware market.

The Gretzky Concept

In order to make strategic decisions about where the company would ultimately go, what markets they would target, and how they would reach that market, they had to fully understand the landscape as it was, and how it had been for centuries. After looking at the data, Fairbank and Morris had little interest in preserving the status quo. In fact, when he talks about his company's approach to strategy, Fairbank, an avid hockey enthusiast calls it, not surprisingly, the Gretzky Concept. "If you go to where the puck is going instead of where it is, it is a lot easier."[2] It was more than just offering teaser rates, zero-interest balance transfers. Rather, he wanted to deeply understand customer's spending habits and use this information to not just help them, but help the company's own growth as well. Also, in order to be successful, he knew as a lending institution he wanted to be what he describes as a "hybrid institution," one that both excels at being a major bank that can take advantage of huge pools of credit risk data and the cost benefits inherent in being a large institution, while at the same creating a strong community based on relationships that smaller, local banks are so successful at.

> **He wanted to deeply understand customer's spending habits and use this information to not just help them, but help the company's own growth as well.**

If Capital One was going to have any chance at success it had to grow and scale to be large enough to pass on the cost benefits of large institutions, while at the same time not losing the personal touch that consumers crave. Some may argue that it isn't really any different than what every other major bank is trying to do. There are countless ads on television and online that promote large banks who "care" about the customer. Some critics and analysts have been vocal about Capital One's claims to care about the customer or have a better understanding of customer needs than any other bank based on data alone. Meredith A. Whitney, a banking analyst at CIBC World Markets, argues, "There is zero evidence that Cap One has a better understanding of retail banking than anyone else. There is no amount of strategy that can battle a flat yield curve."[3]

However, over the years, the data actually has said otherwise. Capital One must be on to something when it comes to their strategy when dealing with customers and understanding their needs. Analyst David George from A.G. Edwards, argues, "They have been better at managing credit risk than many of their peers."[4] They have consistently grown and expanded their market share since 1994 and in an independent industry-wide market research study conducted by Market Force Information in 2017, Capital One was considered consumers' favorite bank and lending institution—beating out all other major banks. More than 6,500 bank customers were polled for the study, and the study provided insights into banking trends, bank technology adoption, and credit card usage.[5]

This, however, raises an important question: how did Capital One grow and expand so quickly, not just compete with, but even surpass its older, more established Visigoth-like competitors? One could argue timing played a key role. It was the nineties. Young people just heading off to college or starting their careers had spent their childhoods immersed in the prosperous and ad-rich eighties. Instant gratification, flashy colors, over-the-top toy commercials promoting everything from sugary-cereals to the latest toy craze—*Cabbage Patch Kids anyone?*—were a way of life. Customization was everything too. Having a bike license plate with your own name it was what all the cool kids were doing. Everyone wanted everything: Fast. One-hour photo labs were the Instagram of yesteryear. You could be at a party, take some photos, and be able to look at the photos before the party ended. Mind-blowing in its day. There was something in the Zeitgeist of the nineties that was prime for Capital One's unique approach to consumers. *Consumers were telling them what they wanted.* Consumers wanted choices. They wanted to feel unique—individual and special. They wanted things to be customized. They also wanted a say in the matter—in all matters. They had opinions and wanted to share them. They weren't their parents or their parents' parents.

While some might argue that the methods Capital One used to attract new customers and ultimately dominate the market share so quickly seemed inconsequential or a fluke, they were in fact critical to the success and extremely calculated. Something as simple as giving cardholders the ability to design their cards—with say their favorite sports' team's logo or their alma mater, had deep psychological effects. It gave the owners of the card a deep and fulfilling sense of pride, a sense of "specialness," and even a sense of belonging. The data showed it also resulted in more frequent spending.

Aggressively marketing was a key strategy. Capital One was virtually omnipresent. It wasn't just the Visigoth ads that garnered attention. They had billboards. Ads in magazines. They deployed sales agents to college campuses. (Full disclosure: This writer's first credit card was a Capital One card—and I believe I selected a van Gogh print for my card that matched a poster in my dorm room.) They specifically sought out those who would otherwise be denied credit because of their lack of credit history. In 2002, they cut a deal with the US Postal Services for bulk mailing and sent an unprecedented number of direct mailings out that offered competitive teaser rates, lower APR, and more options. All of their efforts paid off. In less than a decade they dominated the credit market.

> In 2002, they cut a deal with the US Postal Services for bulk mailing and sent an unprecedented number of direct mailings out that offered competitive teaser rates, lower APR, and more options. All of their efforts paid off. In less than a decade they dominated the credit market.

Expanding Beyond Plastic

Early on before even launching their "What's in your wallet?" campaign, Capital One had their eyes on other markets that also needed to be overhauled and updated. Since the beginning, the company had research teams looking at all manners of consumer lending, and one of those areas was how consumers were paying for their cars. At the time, Capital One was already the ninth-largest credit card issuer—having grown and expanded their market reach considerably since going public in

1994. Then in 1998, they announced they had agreed to buy the privately held Summit Acceptance Corporation, a Dallas-based auto finance company specializing in loans to consumers with troubled credit histories for about $55 million in stock. The acquisition would give Capital One about $260 million in serviced loans. Capital One believed that the purchase would have no short-term effects on its earning per share in 1998, but predicted it would eventually add to them in 1999.[6]

Throughout the early years of the company, Capital One focused on consumer data—looking at trends and opportunities in the marketplace and that data pointed not just to credit cards and auto loans, but insurance, and even phone services and vacation clubs. Not all were success stories. In the beginning, Fairbank and Morris viewed themselves more as a "data-driven marketer" than a finance company. So early on they thought they could apply their data-driven marketing in other fields—like the cellular phone service business.

> **Throughout the early years of the company, Capital One focused on consumer data— looking at trends and opportunities in the marketplace and that data pointed not just to credit cards and auto loans, but insurance, and even phone services and vacation clubs. Not all were success stories.**

It was the height of the technology and telecommunications boom. Fairbank, once described mobile phones as "credit cards with antennae."[7] But the business, called America One, never got off the ground. It was too small and couldn't offer competitive pricing that other major players could. Fairbank cut his losses and sold their remaining accounts to Sprint Corp. "It was too tall an order for us. It was a strategic failure on my part," Fairbank admits.[8] But, it was a learning experience in the highest order and it convinced him to dial back their diversifications, and instead focus singularly on auto lending and international consumer finance.

Rallying after Failure

At the height of the launch of their successful "What's in your wallet?" campaign the company experienced what Morris called extreme "velocity." They were taking off and looking for ways to expand even further. In 2001, Capital One acquired PeopleFirst, Inc., the nation's largest online provider of direct motor vehicle loans. This acquisition would make Capital One one of the nation's largest providers of D2C loans. In a Capital One issued press release, Fairbank explained the reason for the acquisition was more than just to expand the market. Rather, he was looking toward the future and how people were engaging in borrowing—specifically online. "Leveraging People-First's successful online business model with Capital One's proven ability to customize products will ultimately benefit auto buyers nationwide. With the acquisition of PeopleFirst, Capital One extends its auto finance strategy to superprime consumers and those directly seeking flexible financing online," Fairbank said.[9]

At the time, PeopleFirst Inc. was a privately held company with more than 270 employees based in San Diego, CA. With the acquisition it became a wholly owned subsidiary of Capital One. After the acquisition, the current senior team at People-First continued to manage its operations and were optimistic about the venture. In the press release, Gary Miller, then CEO and cofounder of PeopleFirst, said "We are excited to become part of the Capital One family. Not only does Capital One bring significant resources and opportunities for PeopleFirst to leverage, but they also share our strong commitment to customers."[10]

Just two years later, PeopleFirst was absorbed completely into Capital One and rebranded as Capital One Auto Finance Corporation. The move included a new website address, www.capitaloneautofinance.com, and it promised to offer consumers access to vehicle loans across the full credit spectrum. In addition to offering dealer and direct-mail auto financing programs, Capital One Auto Finance could now also provide the "convenience, ease and value" of PeopleFirst's direct-to-consumer *online* auto loans. In a Capital One press release, Dave Lawson, Capital One Auto Finance CEO, said "By combining our talents and unique expertise, we have developed successful, integrated lending solutions that deliver low rate loans across the full credit spectrum. By marketing our Internet, direct mail and dealer channels under a single banner we now have unprecedented depth in the auto finance marketplace and can offer consumers the best service—and some of the most competitive rates—online."[11] Brian Reed, then-president of PeopleFirst, said "We've revolutionized auto lending by leveraging the web to provide outstanding consumer value, a hassle-free process and dynamic customer service. Our dedication to putting people first has allowed us to grow from an Internet start-up to an integral part of Capital One's financial services portfolio. So, while our Internet address has changed, our customer commitment is stronger than ever and our ability to serve and grow has been enhanced by Capital One."[12]

Taking Advantage of Opportunities in the Market

By July 2003, as the company was expanding into other markets, interest rates had hit historic lows. Many consumers throughout the country were able to take advantage of record-low interest rates on everything from mortgages, student loans, to new car loans. Capital One made a bold move. They announced a new kind of credit card that would offer a *fixed* 4.99 percent rate credit card. This was not only unheard of, but unprecedented. It was not a teaser rate or introductory rate. It would be the lowest long-term fixed interest rate in the nation for both purchases and balance transfers. The 4.99 percent fixed interest rate offered customers with excellent credit histories an opportunity to save money and increase their purchasing power using the best priced credit card available in the US market. The card joined a long list of competitive product offerings from Capital One that include a range of rewards and low pricing features designed to meet the needs of individual consumers. In a Capital One press release, Diana Don, spokesperson for Capital One, said "The financial services industry is seeing increased consumer demand across the board for competitive interest rates. Whether they're looking for a mortgage, an auto loan, or a credit card, comparison shopping is important. Looking for the best rate and terms available can save consumers money. Capital One's long-term fixed interest rate credit card will benefit consumers with established credit who are paying higher interest rate fees than necessary and provide them with a more affordable option for credit purchases."[13]

In addition to the cost savings of a low interest rate, Capital One was also offering no balance transfer or cash advance fees, no annual fee, zero liability for fraudulent or unauthorized charges (online or off), and customized payment dates. Consumers who qualified for Capital One's new Platinum MasterCard® would be enjoying one of the most consumer-friendly credit cards ever issued by a major US bank. Anyone could apply for the card at a catchy website named: www.getmycard.com. Again the emphasis was on "my" card—personalized, and just for "me."

> **Capital One made a bold move. They announced a new kind of credit card that would offer a *fixed* 4.99 percent rate credit card. This was not only unheard of, but unprecedented. It was not a teaser rate or introductory rate. It would be the lowest long-term fixed interest rate in the nation for both purchases and balance transfers.**

Thanks in part to the acquisitions, a dominant online presence, and low-interest rates, Capital One enjoyed success. By the second quarter of 2003, they announced that their earnings per share had increased by *34 percent* over the same period in the prior year. Earnings for the second quarter of 2003 were

$286.8 million, or $1.23 per share (fully diluted) compared with earnings of $213.1 million, or $0.92 per share, for the second quarter of 2002. Earnings in the first quarter of 2003 were $309.1 million, or $1.35 per share. In addition to the increased earnings, they were seeing improvements in all manners of business. The managed charge-off (accounts that customers could not pay) had declined to 6.32 percent in the second quarter of 2003, from 6.47 percent in the previous quarter. The managed delinquency rate declined to 4.95 percent from 4.97 percent at the end of the previous quarter. In a Capital One press release that year, David R. Lawson, Capital One's then chief financial officer, said, "We continue to expect managed loan growth of 15 to 20 percent in 2003. Our diversified efforts in auto finance and international will be an increasing contributor to the earnings growth of Capital One this year."[14]

What was truly astounding was just how much the company was investing in marketing at the time. Marketing expenses for the second quarter of 2003 increased $28.9 million to $270.6 million from $241.7 million in the first quarter. However, it was down from what he had spent the previous year: a whopping $320.4 million in the comparable period of the prior year. No other credit card could compete with their market domination.

Looking Out for the Consumer

With the rise of online banking there was a new existential threat to both credit card companies, banks, and consumers alike: identity theft. Between 1998–2004 over 27 million Americans became victims of identity theft. The main means of identity theft was credit card fraud. Capital One went back to its roots—what made them so successful was looking at the data, finding out what was going on in the market, and then educating the consumer. To help combat the growing issue that could have devastating consequences to consumers, Capital One joined with an unlikely partner to take on identity theft: an author. Robert Hammond, author of *Identity Theft: How to Protect Your Most Valuable Asset*, teamed up with Capital One to raise awareness and inform American consumers on how to prevent identity theft as well as what to do if it should happen to them. Since Capital One offered its customers a 100 percent guarantee against fraud protection, it was, of course, in their own interest as well to educate consumers.

While some of the information that Hammond and Capital One shared seems like common sense today, it was news to most people. The belief then was that identity theft was committed just by anonymous hackers. But, in reality, many individuals who reported identity theft were victimized by someone they knew—family members, friends or neighbors, and work associates. Hammond and Capital One encouraged consumers to be wary of others. They advised "never leave credit cards, credit card bills, or solicitations lying around—keep them in a safe place, or better yet, shred them."[15]

They also advised password protection. Of course, identity theft software and programs are much more sophisticated and common these days, but back then they were not. Capital One was on the vanguard of educating its own consumers and took an active interest in their financial health and safety. Showing they cared for and had their customers' backs with the 100 percent fraud protection guarantee endeared them to the market. They encouraged consumers to take action—reporting back to creditors so that fraudulent accounts could be closed. They encouraged consumers to monitor their own credit—checking in with the three national credit reporting agencies,

Equifax, Experian, and TransUnion. They also encouraged rigorous record keeping—obtaining credit reports and ensuring no additional accounts could be opened in one's name and sending disputes in writing as well. They advised keeping and tracking details of all the correspondence and created an "Identity Theft Fraud Action Tracking Sheet" for consumers who had become victims.

> **Capital One was on the vanguard of educating its own consumers and took an active interest in their financial health and safety. Showing they cared for and had their customers' backs with the 100 percent fraud protection guarantee endeared them to the market.**

Capital One was one of the first to take a proactive approach to educating consumers, and they did so by relying on data and surveys. In a cosponsored survey with the consumer advocacy group Consumer Action, Capital One learned that a growing segment of the population in desperate need of understanding their own financials was teenagers. Why would Capital One take an interest in consumers who aren't age-eligible to carry credit cards? One could argue it was yet another Gretzky-type play by Fairbank to get out ahead of the puck and see where the market was headed.

Capital One was very interested in the disparate mindsets of generations when it came to how each generation related to money. According to the survey of parents and their teenaged children, more than half of the parents said they thought their teens' knowledge of money management was "good to excellent" however, 78 percent of the teens said their understanding was "average or even poor." What the survey also revealed was that parents really weren't talking in depth to their teens about cash, credit, and money management as a whole. Thus, the opportunity to educate the future market and potential customers became yet another strategic play.

In 2003, Consumer Action and Capital One partnered to develop a free workbook called *Talking to Teens about Money*, which included activities, worksheets, and samples designed to guide teens and parents through a discussion of money management basics. Diana Don, then director of Financial Education at Capital One, said, "Good money management is not something that is routinely taught in schools so it is important for teenagers to learn these skills at home. *Talking to Teens about Money* can help parents by leading their teens through very specific exercises that show how credit ratings are built and how they can be damaged, how checking accounts work and how developing a budget can help keep teens from overspending."

Talking to Teens about Money was just one part of the "Money-Wise" program which Capital One launched in 2001 with Consumer Action as a national financial literacy campaign. It was the first program of its kind to combine "free, multilingual financial education materials with community training and seminars to give consumers at all income levels both the information and the practical assistance they need to make smart financial choices."[16] In addition the partnership also provided free financial training seminars to more than 80 nonprofit community groups from across the Washington, DC, metro area. The two-day seminar focused six areas of financial management for clients of community groups: banking, budgeting, understanding credit, credit repair, understanding bankruptcy, and talking to teens about money.[17]

> **In a cosponsored survey with the consumer advocacy group Consumer Action, Capital One learned that a growing segment of the population in desperate need of understanding their own financials was teenagers.**

While this was largely proactive, it was also a response to the growing economic crisis. In 2003, the US was experiencing continued high unemployment rates. Experts were predicting an even worsening economy. Household debt was also increasing and the number of personal bankruptcies in the US was continuing to rise. It was clear to Capital One that the majority of Americans were woefully uninformed. Capital One and Consumer Action wanted to help them make better financial choices and decisions. In response they released a guide, *Your Right to a Financial Fresh Start,* that detailed the pros and cons of bankruptcy, the legal process, and other resources that would benefit them while in the process of making such a major decision. Capital One was not advocating bankruptcy,[18] however, as a creditor directly impacted by bankruptcy, they had a vested interest in the financial health of their potential customers. In response they wanted to educate the public about the impact bankruptcies can have on their financial future, reminding them that bankruptcies have a long-term impact. By March the following year they launched the MoneyWise website (www .money-wise.org) as a way to a provide free access to a full array of unbiased financial education resources.[19]

Expanding Offerings Despite the Downturn

Despite the economic slump, unemployment on the rise, and rising household debt, Capital One doubled down on new credit card offerings, launching their New Go Miles Card, which offered travelers "No Hassle Rewards." It was a new airline travel credit card, that unlike other cards that offered airline miles, customers could use the miles they earned when and how they wanted. Again, responding to consumers' needs and requests, Capital One was now offering no blackout dates and the freedom to choose any airline (as opposed to airline loyalty card issuers), which would then allow consumers to comparison shop and get the lowest fares. In addition, consumers could use the miles to purchase the tickets any way they preferred—through a travel agent, online, or directly from the preferred airline. As a further incentive they offered 5,000 free miles for balance transfers, an introductory APR of 9.9 percent, and a $19 annual fee. The purpose of the card was twofold: Reward costumers who were loyal to Capital One and empower them to make cost-saving decisions by choosing the right fares for themselves.[20] It continued to roll out new offerings throughout 2004 and continued to expand their stake in the credit card market.

End of the Startup Era

While Capital One continued to grow and expand in its first ten years, despite 9/11 and a declining economy, it faced one considerable challenge that would impede its fast-paced growth and it showed it was no longer in startup mode: It had caught the attention of the regulators. In the earnings report that Capital One issued on July 16, 2002, it revealed that after a routine regulatory review, the company and its subsidiaries would expect to enter into an "informal memorandum of understanding with bank regulators addressing certain regulatory matters." Federal and state banking regulators questioned the company's model for assessing credit risk. And in 2003, chief financial officer David M. Willy was forced to resign after the Securities and Exchange Commission notified him that he was being investigated for insider trading. Though charges were not brought against him, it made investors balk. Capital One shares sank to a five-year low.

However, in January 2004, the Federal Reserve Bank of Richmond, the Office of Thrift Supervision, and the Bureau of Financial Institutions of the Commonwealth of Virginia terminated the memorandum of understanding (MOU), which expresses a convergence of will between all parties, indicating an intended common line of action.[21] The stock soared at around $71, up 180 percent from the previous year. Over time it became abundantly clear that the regulators' worst fears about Capital One were largely baseless. Each year their bad-loan charge-offs gradually dropped, and earnings per share rose 23 percent in 2003.[22]

But the leaders of Capital One thought it was time to rethink their management style. They were entering a new era. They were no longer a startup company and they could no longer manage like one. Morris acknowledged this and said in an interview with Bloomberg Business at the time, "Capital One is a big company. We need to govern in a way consistent with that. You can't have two guys driving up I-95 in a black Ford making business decisions. It just doesn't work anymore." Of course, Morris was referring to how he and Fairbank thought through major issues when working together at Signet in the early years.

As a result of the regulators' concerns, Fairbank created an executive team that began to meet with him each Monday to help formulate strategy in a consistent and transparent way. It wasn't just two guys in a sedan making major decisions for the company, though in truth, it hadn't been that way for some time. In the same Bloomberg article, analyst Vincent Daniel said, "I hate to use the 'b' word on them, but it's a little more bureaucratic. And to a certain extent it needed to be. Bank regulators don't necessarily want an extremely entrepreneurial culture."[23]

One person who felt the tightening grip of the new corporate culture was Morris. In 2003, he announced he would leave the company in 2004 and step down from his role as president, becoming instead a vice chairman. Morris wanted to pursue other interests and missed the startup entrepreneurial energy that fueled the early years of Capital One. With Fairbank at the helm, Capital One began to look more like a "traditional bank."[24] While it began as a company that focused on "subprime" borrowers—or those with thin files who tended to be more high risk—the new era was going to call for something different, like focusing on lending more to more low-risk credit-worthy individuals.

"The brush with regulators left a lasting mark on Cap One's customer base," wrote Nanette Byrnes for Bloomberg. Fairbank needed to respond to that risk and make adjustments. If he were to change course, and do less lending to "subprime" borrowers and more lending to the A-list of credit quality, he would be faced with a lot more competition. Another answer to the question of how to increase growth was to look beyond credit cards and loans. Though its bread and butter had been direct-mail credit-card solicitation and auto loans, Capital One knew it was time to look beyond credit and into traditional retail banking. "It's one of the missing puzzle pieces to being a diversified consumer finance institution," Fairbank told Byrnes in 2004 in a rare showing of his strategic hand. Retail banking was a long way from the startup Capital One's initial strategy, but growth happens and so do the changing needs of the consumer and the demands of the marketplace.

It was time for a new strategy, the puck was on the move, and Fairbank, alone now, was going to have to get there before anyone else.

"I have always believed that the choices a company makes during the good times will determine its fate during the bad times."

—RICHARD FAIRBANK

CHAPTER THREE

FROM STARTUP ERA TO RECESSION TO TOO BIG TO FAIL

After Morris left, Fairbank and Capital One's executives set their sights where their competition had always dominated: mortgages and branch banking. It was a calculated risk. Just as he approached all risk, Fairbank looked at the numbers. The opportunity was there. And unlike when they started in business, they had a track record and proven success. They had beaten legacy banks in the credit card game, so why couldn't they beat them at everything else using the same data-mining approach. A year after Morris's departure, Capital purchased New Orleans-based Hibernia National Bank for $5 billion and later that year, it was the Melville, New York's North Fork Bancorp. To outsiders and investors, it looked a smart move; Fairbank was consolidating small branches and bringing them under the Capital One fold. But, of course, there were vocal critics too.

> **"** To outsiders and investors, it looked a smart move; Fairbank was consolidating small branches and bringing them under the Capital One fold. But, of course, there were vocal critics too.

The Perfect Storm

But just as timing worked in his favor in the early nineties when launching the business, it worked against him this go around. Just as he was about to sign the Hibernia deal in the summer of 2005, Hurricane Katrina slammed onto New Orleans's coastline—decimating the bank's home territory. This prompted a $186 million charge against its holdings and trimmed the cost of the sale price by $400 million.[1] According to *Institutional Investor*, "It rendered 120 of Hibernia's 317 branches inoperable. Katrina, the costliest natural disaster in US history, displaced nearly half of Hibernia's 6,500 employees, including Louisiana banking chief Paul Bonitatibus, who lived for seven months in hotels and motels after his home in Jefferson Parish was flooded."[2] To their credit, Hibernia put hundreds of other employees up in temporary housing while the area rebuilt. Then, three weeks later, Hurricane Rita struck western Louisiana and Texas and forced the bank to evacuate and temporarily close an additional 60 branches. Dark days indeed were ahead.

At the time Fairbank was also working on a deal with North Fork's mortgage unit. It was about the same time the US housing market started to dip for the first time in years. It was not a good time to get into the mortgage business. "Mortgage origination in the US fell by 16 percent during the first half of 2006, and a flat-to-inverted yield curve was squeezing banking industry margins. North Fork's earnings fell 14 percent in the third quarter, strongly disappointing Wall Street," reported Loren Fox for *Institutional Investor* in January of 2007, completely unaware of course, that the worst was yet to come for banks.[3]

But prior to the crash, Capital One was feeling the pinch. Their shares began to drop. Analysts and shareholders alike criticized Fairbank. "They shouldn't have bought North Fork so close on the heels of Hibernia and with the impending changes in the mortgage business," Credit Suisse analyst Moshe Orenbuch argued. "In the short term it was executed in a way that hurt the shareholders."[4] But, Fairbank didn't agree, saying, "We clearly took more short-term risk for the long-term benefit of doing a transformational deal."[5]

Some of Fairbank's harshest critics thought he should have just sold the company outright. He wouldn't have been alone. Other credit card competitors had done just that—they chose to be bought up by major banks, handsomely rewarding stockholders in the process. But Fairbank was in for the long game. The wave of consolidation was triggered, *Institutional Investor* says, "by slowing growth in cards as consumers paid off balances and used plastic less after a decade long binge."[6] At the time, the revolving consumer credit outstanding in the US was at $863 billion, according to Federal Reserve Board data. Capital One's earnings were beginning to slow—having only risen 18 percent in 2005, after enjoying average annual gain of 35 percent in the previous three years. Borrowing was slowing down, largely because people were maxed out—figuratively and literally. Fairbank knew he had to look for opportunity elsewhere. He had already taken on auto loans, and it made sense that mortgages were next. They had over the past decade grown an average of seven percent or more per year, compared with just 3 to 4 percent for cards.[7]

Even before the crash and even before the subprime mortgage crisis, Fairbank had a sense things were shifting in the banking industry. He predicted that banking would be "dominated by a handful of big national players instead of an array of local entrants. For the small number of players who position themselves as a consolidator, there's a very significant growth opportunity here."[8]

Though Fairbank couldn't predict the stock market crash of 2008, he seemed to recognize the subprime time bomb that was North Fork's Greenpoint Mortgage unit, a national mortgage and home equity lender, actually was. Even if others couldn't. As soon as he got a look at North Fork's books, he planned to shut Greenpoint down. In now what seems like a totally ironic statement, Bruce Harting, an analyst from the now-defunct Lehman brothers, said of Capital One's acquisition of North Fork (and thereby Greenpoint) in 2007, "In many ways this is a marriage made in heaven."[9] Fairbank didn't agree. In an August 2007 press release, it said Capital One was officially ceasing residential mortgage origination operations in its wholesale mortgage banking unit, Greenpoint Mortgage, "effective immediately" citing "current conditions in the secondary mortgage markets create significant near-team profitability challenges, given the company's 'originate and sell' business model. Further, recent and continuing developments in the mortgage markets reduce the long-term outlook for profitability in the business, as the company expects markets for prime, non-conforming mortgage products are like to remain challenged for the foreseeable future."[10] Along with this decision it closed Greenpoint's California-based headquarters along with 31 locations in 19 states, and eliminated approximately 1,900 positions. It was sobering and devastating news for employees and for markets. It was also prescient. In a year, the entire market would come crashing down.

Capital One Faces the Worst Economy Since the Great Depression

Fairbank was still focused as ever as Capital One began to target other aspects of traditional retail banking. But if he was going to enter this arena, he was going to enter it much like he did the credit business—with one eye on innovation and another on doing things completely differently than they had ever been done before. The long-term plan was to keep buying banks and building scale to compete with industry giants. All along Fairbank was in it for the long game, though he had his fair share of doubters. At the time, some believed Capital One was prime for takeover. Peter Kovalski, manager of the Alpine Dynamic Financial services funds, and then a shareholder, admitted to the *Institutional Investor*, that "They're not in a position where they need to sell, but I still consider it a takeover candidate." Fairbank was unmoved by detractors or doubters. "I have 18 years of experience competing against the big players."[11]

All along Fairbank believed that banking was "ripe for reinvention" and that's why he got in the game in the first place. But dark days were ahead for all banks and lending institutions, and let's not forget Americans in general. Yet, despite what seemed like an atomic meltdown across the US as it headed into a recession, Capital One came out largely unscathed. In a press release dated October 16, 2008, just a little over two weeks after the stock market crash, Fairbank came out and assured stockholders all was well within the company, stating, "Against the backdrop of increasing economic headwinds and unprecedented change in the financial services landscape, Capital One continues to deliver profits and generate capital. But we are not complacent. Based on what we're seeing in the world around us, we are significantly increasing the intensity of our efforts to aggressively manage the company for the benefit of investors and customers through the current downturn."[12]

Gary L. Perlin, Capital One's chief financial officer at the time, went so far as to say the company had "a rock solid balance sheet through the recession." Adding, "Our capital ratios are comfortably above our targets and our readily available liquidity is more than four times our debt refinancing needs for the next year, positioning us not only to navigate this storm but also to capitalize on financially attractive opportunities when they arise."[13]

However, it may have been too soon to see the massive fallout that the crash actually had. In his 2008 letter preceding the Annual Report, Fairbank's report was decidedly more sobering, "In 2008, it became clear that banks were facing the worst financial crisis since the Great Depression. Housing values plummeted. The capital markets froze. Unemployment escalated. Consumers lost confidence. The federal government pumped large sums of money into the financial system broadly and into banks themselves. Many of the nation's largest banks were ravaged by the recession as they struggled to manage their capital, liquidity, and losses."[14]

Dealing with the Fallout of 2008

In order to deal with fallout, Fairbank focused on what he called, "two critical imperatives." Which, according to him, were, "First, we hunkered down to weather the economic storm, aggressively managing credit risk and building an even stronger balance sheet. Second, we continued to position the company to compete and win on the other side of the recession. Every action in our company worked backwards from these two critical objectives."[15] He went on to say that in fact Capital One's financial performance did ultimately suffer in the midst of the economic crisis.

While just two weeks after the crisis they had reported increases, by the end of the year the story changed dramatically. Fairbank writes, "Capital One's net operating income in 2008 was $895 million, or $2.28 per share, not including a non-cash goodwill write-down of $811 million associated with the shrinking of our auto finance business. Total company earnings, including the goodwill write-down and the impacts of discontinued operations and restructuring costs, were negative for the year at ($46) million, or ($0.21) per share. Our earnings reflected significant declines year-over-year, primarily driven by higher charge-offs across our lending businesses and the degradation of our economic outlook for the next 12 months, which caused us to add just over $1.5 billion to our allowance for loan losses in anticipation of increasing charge-offs in 2009."[16]

Despite the losses, though, Fairbank assured shareholders that over all Capital One had performed well in 2008 on a relative basis, "with our total shareholder return finishing in the top 20 percent of the S&P financials."[17]

Despite the challenging economy, Fairbank asserted that 2008 was also a year of progress for Capital One. He credits that to the many strategic choices they had made over the years, which he says were "validated when tested by the economic storm."[18] These critical decisions included their business mix, banking transformation, decreased reliance on capital markets funding, capital and liquidity strategies, and early exit from the GreenPoint Mortgage origination business, which was inherited as part of the North Fork Bank acquisition. It also raised $761 million of common equity in the public equity markets, strengthening its balance sheet and providing Capital One with the flexibility to take advantage of attractive opportunities during the downturn. Fairbank reported, "Our balance sheet remained strong, with $40 billion of immediately available liquidity and a tangible common equity (TCE) ratio of 5.6 percent at year-end. And, on the asset side of our balance sheet, we avoided many of the significant exposures and risks that other banks have experienced, including assets which lead to large, sudden, and unexpected mark-to-market write-downs."[19]

Despite the challenging economy, Fairbank asserted that 2008 was also a year of progress for Capital One. He credits that to the many strategic choices they had made over the years, which he says were "validated when tested by the economic storm."

Fairbank was assuring investors that the fundamentals of their credit card and banking businesses remained solid and reported how in the year of a massive downturn the US card continued to deliver strong returns on a risk-adjusted basis and still managed to generate $1 billion of net income and $1.7 billion of capital. The company grew total deposits by 32 percent and expanded the net interest margin, despite the increasingly competitive deposit market. The total deposits at year-end totaled $109 billion and it put them squarely on the Top Ten List of banks—they were now the eighth largest bank in the United States.

In addition to solid growth, they began aggressive cost-cutting measures, reducing their operating expenses by $445 million. Fairbank credits this to what he called, "disciplined expense management" adding that it had been a "key component of offsetting rising credit losses and driving shareholder value."[20]

Taking Advantage of Opportunities in the Downturn

Looking to diversify, they were ready to make the move into retail banking. Just two months after the crash in December of 2008, Capital One announced the acquisition of Chevy Chase Bank, a leading bank in the Washington, DC, area, for $520 million. The transaction was completed in the first quarter of 2009. At the time Chevy Chase Bank was the leading banking franchise in the Washington, DC, area, which was also Capital One's corporate headquarters and hometown. Fairbank believed that Washington, DC, was a "strong and resilient banking market." It was the ninth largest metro area in the country by population, with above average population growth. At the time it boasted the highest per capita income and lowest unemployment rate among the top 20 metro areas in the United States.

Fairbank said of the acquisition, "We are glad that Chevy Chase Bank will stay locally owned and that Washington, DC, will remain the home of one of the nation's top 10 banks." Chevy Chase Bank had a dominant local market position, with branches on what Fairbank called the "best corners." It had the number one branch share in the Washington, DC, area, with 244 branches and over 1,000 ATMs. Chevy Chase Bank ranked number five in deposit share, with $13.5 billion in deposits, having focused on investing in many new branches. Fairbank was enthusiastic about the purchase and said, "This franchise is a coiled spring with plenty of untapped upside potential."[21]

As Capital One neared 2009, they were approaching their fifteenth anniversary as a company. Despite the economic downturn, they had 35 million customers and boasted "one of the nation's most recognizable brands, with 99 percent total brand awareness."

Why would Capital One acquire a local DC branch banking business? Fairbank explained it was to ultimately improve their deposit funding base and expand their portfolio of local banking franchises, while adding scale to their banking operations. But, it was also a strategic branding move. As Capital One neared 2009, they were approaching their fifteenth anniversary as a company. Despite the economic downturn, they had 35 million customers and boasted "one of the nation's most recognizable brands, with 99 percent total brand awareness."[22] Having invested in building the brand and delivering industry-leading television ads and marketing creative for many years, Fairbank had plenty of reasons to believe that Capital One's brand investments were paying off. Fairbank explained, "Our brand is a significant differentiator for us against the other big banks, and well beyond the reach of the thousands of smaller banks in the country. While we often feature credit cards in our signature national advertising, our brand is not limited to national lending."

He believed the power of the Capital One brand would ultimately extend directly to local banking. Fairbank further clarified, "Brand awareness and brand consideration in the New York market increased significantly when we re-branded North Fork Bank branches as Capital One Bank, and bumped even higher when we introduced Capital One Bank television advertising and other trade area marketing in the New York area." Fairbank was well aware that brand was not simply about television advertising though. "Ultimately, our brand is only as good as the underlying reality when customers experience our products and service."[23]

> ❝ Ultimately, our brand is only as good as the underlying reality when customers experience our products and service."

Fairbank was well aware of what his customers expected—great value and convenience every time they transact with

Capital One "on any product, anytime, anywhere." Whether it was with a credit card, opening a savings account, operating online or in a branch, Fairbank was committed to meeting his customers' high expectations.

Preparing for the Bad Times

Perhaps Fairbank's biggest tool in the toolbox when dealing with the economic meltdown was preparation. Fairbank says, "I have always believed that the choices a company makes during the good times will determine its fate during the bad times. From our inception as a company, we have chosen a conservative path with respect to our business mix, credit risk management, and balance sheet management to position our company to be as resilient as possible during both good times and bad. We have always operated on the premise that the future could be worse than the past and that a recession could start tomorrow, rigorously focusing for years on building a company to weather a severe downturn."[24]

Fairbank essentially made a wager: "On the other side of the recession, we believe that there will be a revaluation of banks and their business models, and that the winners will be disproportionately rewarded." He believed that the conservative choices Capital One had built their business on would ultimately pay off for their investors. He went on to explain that this was largely because the banking transformation and business mix provided resiliency. As a public company, Capital One started as a specialty credit card lender and rapidly leveraged their growth and diversified into other areas of consumer banking, while largely avoiding less resilient businesses, like mortgages.

During this period, however, Fairbank acknowledged, the specialty lending business model was becoming an industry standard. He believed that this business model's overreliance on capital markets funding made it potentially vulnerable. "In good times," Fairbank concluded, "the capital markets are an efficient funding source. But in bad times, we believed an economic downturn could create funding challenges during an extended period of capital markets dislocation. Funding is like oxygen. Having it 98 percent of the time just isn't good enough." That is why he planned from the outset to reduce their dependence on the capital markets through the acquisition of banking markets in order to provide the stability of deposit funding and to position the company for long-term profitable growth.

As previously mentioned, the move was initially criticized by outsiders. Capital One's acquisition of Hibernia Bank, the largest bank in Louisiana with a growing presence in top markets in Texas, and then North Fork Bank in 2006, both seemed ill-timed at the outset—first because of Katrina and then because of the subprime financial crisis. But Fairbank was a step ahead of the critics and naysayers. "Our move into local banking was well timed. The capital markets began to close down following the subprime mortgage meltdown in April of 2007 and have been largely shut ever since. Financial companies without access to retail deposits have faced funding challenges in the grips of a ferocious economy. In addition, our entry into banking purposely concentrated the company's businesses in two of the most profitable and resilient parts of banking— credit cards and deposits. Our choices are serving us well."[25]

While no bank—or business,—for that matter—is immune to cyclical economic forces, Capital One seemed to be because of their carefully chosen business mix, expansion into banking, avoidance of risky investments, and insulation from capital markets volatility.

Dealing with Customers Going Through Hard Times

That being said, Capital One was well aware that at the core of their business were customers who were reeling from the recession: customers who lost their jobs, their money, or retirement funds and found themselves in the unfortunate position of struggling to pay their bills. Again, Capital One planned for this. "For two decades, we have hardwired severe economic worsening assumptions into our underwriting processes, building our company to weather a substantial economic downturn and thrive on the other side," Fairbank said. But, given the downturn they were also adapting models and processes in real time, tightening underwriting and aggressively intervening where credit performance warranted it.

In the annual report of that year, Fairbank assured investors that they weren't going to let delinquent accounts slide: "We are continuing our intense focus on the collection and recovery of bad loans, with earlier contact of delinquent customers, higher intensity, and new tools to help customers get back on track." And in commercial banking, he reorganized—deploying staff from lending operations to handle the increase in bank-owned properties. All of this is to say: *People were losing their homes. People were losing their jobs. People were unable to pay their bills and were in crisis.* While Fairbank was well aware he needed to assure investors that Capital One was doing everything in their power to maintain the business, he was quick to point out that he hadn't forgotten the real people behind his business: *the customers.* It wasn't just about improving credit models and ramping up collections, he said, but "It is also about treating customers who find themselves in difficulty with humanity and respect."[26] Capital One had always had a customer hardship program, but in 2008 it implemented more enhanced interest waivers, interest rate reductions, as well as other steps to help customers meet their debt obligations. In Fairbank's mind, "Finding collaborative ways to solve customers' problems by identifying solutions that accommodate their individual circumstances is a win for everyone."[27] His ultimate goal was not, as critics claimed, to make a buck off the poor or downtrodden, it was to help empower customers to get back on their feet, avoid charge-offs (canceling the debts that the customer is unable to pay), and reduce damage to their credit scores. It was also yet another opportunity to fortify Capital One's relationship with the customer as well as to engender trust and customer loyalty.

 While Fairbank was well aware he needed to assure investors that Capital One was doing everything in their power to maintain the business, he was quick to point out that he hadn't forgotten the real people behind his business: *the customers*.

While Capital One wanted to lend to qualified borrowers, and knew that they stood to make money off of the interest on those lines, they also knew that the fundamental premise of disciplined lending was that a customer must be willing and able to pay back the loan. "Making a bad loan hurts the customer, Capital One, and our investors," Fairbank wrote. He would never sacrifice the long-term for a short-term gain. In other words, Capital One would remain selective about the loans they booked throughout the downturn, but they would never lose sight of serving their customers.

So despite the downturn, they invested heavily in improving their customer infrastructure in 2008, including online servicing capabilities with the introduction of mobile banking, transaction and fraud alerts, secure email, and rewards improvements. They also rolled out and made enhancements to their Capital One CardLab—an interactive, online marketplace for credit cards. CardLab allowed customers to select the combination of features most important to them, including interest rates, annual fees, and rewards options. CardLab also enabled customers to personalize their plastics by uploading an image or photo to be displayed on the front of the credit card—whether a favorite family photo or a picture of a beloved pet. Fairbank was quick to acknowledge, "CardLab is a hit with our customers. They love the exceptional value, transparency, convenience, and control."[28]

In 2008, they added to their innovative travel rewards program with the new No Hassle Rewards Card, which offered double miles and maximum flexibility since rewards can be redeemed for any travel-related expenses, such as airlines, hotels, cruise lines, and rental cars. They did the same for our small-business customers, launching a Preferred No Hassle Miles Card that offered *business owners* double rewards on travel and entertainment services.

They also expanded their rewards beyond the credit cards. In 2008, they launched the Capital One Rewards Checking account, a product that enabled customers to earn rewards quickly and easily for everyday banking activities, like shopping at the mall, debit card purchases, cash withdrawals, and paying bills online.

Responding to Regulation Changes

With economic crisis came sweeping changes. In 2008, the Federal Reserve announced a new set of rules regarding lending practices, which were to be implemented across the industry by 2010. While the new rules created substantial costs for most lending institutions, Capital One was able to adapt, and in some cases was completely unaffected. For example, among other practices, the new rules banned the highly criticized practices of double-cycle billing and "universal default" (where issuers increase interest rates because of customer behavior on other loans or changes to credit bureau scores). As far as Fairbank saw it the regulations worked in Capital One's favor. He proudly reported, "We never engaged in many of the banned practices in the first place, including double-cycle billing and universal default. Years ago we voluntarily introduced the most customer-friendly repricing policy in the industry. We already are well down the path of compliance, having made a number of these changes well before the industry was under a spotlight and before the new rules were even contemplated."[29]

Focusing on Employees During the Crisis

While many companies were busy managing layoffs and record high reports of job dissatisfaction, Capital One remained committed to their culture, morale, and showing gratitude for their exceptional workforce. Fairbank stated, "The greatest franchise we have at Capital One is not our credit card franchise or our banking franchise. It is our people. Greatness often is on display during periods of adversity. Our great people at Capital One are facing perhaps the most challenging industry and economic environment in their lifetimes. They are not deterred. They continue to give it their all as they mitigate losses, reposition our businesses, and build for future growth."[30]

Fairbank has often said he believes his most important job as CEO has been "to attract great people and then to create an environment where they can be great." He was openly proud of his employees and boasted of their collective achievements, namely how many of them donated tens of thousands of hours of their time to help their communities. However, Fairbank was quick to add, "our people did not give just their time and money. They also contributed their ingenuity." That year, they continued their ongoing efforts to provided financial education, and this time to children. Working with Junior Achievement, they set up an innovative mobile classroom called "Finance Park" where kids learn how to manage a household budget through very realistic role play. It was, in Fairbank's own words, a "tremendous hit" in Fairfax County in Virginia, where it was required for all 12,000 of its eighth graders. In addition to "Finance Park," Capital One also opened its first fully operational bank branch in a public school at Fordham Leadership Academy in New York. The branch was run by the students and it made such an impact that it was visited by the comptroller of the currency and the head of the FDIC.

Awards and Accolades in the Downturn

Though demurring and hesitant to boast about his own success, Fairbank acknowledged that he does not "judge our company by awards," but rather uses the external recognition to validate things they already know about their culture. In 2008, despite the blows to the banking industry, they were ranked number two in North America and number five globally on *Fortune*'s "Best Companies for Leaders" list. They were also named as one of the most adoption-friendly workplaces in America by the Dave Thomas Foundation for Adoption®, citing their generous adoption reimbursement and parental leave programs. They were ranked as one of the top 50 companies in America for diversity by *DiversityInc*® magazine. LGBTQ organizations continue to recognize them for their "culture and policies." Among those policies were "flexible work" programs, which promote alternative and mobile work arrangements, which were hailed for the flexibility they provide to working families. While other companies were looking to downsize, Capital One was still very committed to investing in employees and creating an environment where they could attract "the brightest and most motivated people from all walks of life" to choose Capital One.[31]

While faced with difficulty and preparing for a severe downturn with virtually unknown outcomes, Fairbank believed wholeheartedly in his company and was sure they were "well positioned to weather the storm." The hallmarks of Capital One's values, Fairbank said were "Excellence" and "Do the Right Thing." And he was sure that by staying true to their values and standing by their principles they would not just endure, but flourish.

Fairbank was right. They indeed weathered the storm. By 2011, they had so fully weathered it they were actively seizing more opportunities for great expansion. However, when they set out to purchase ING Direct USA it unwittingly threw Capital One in the center of a political firestorm. Suddenly the "startup" was smack dab in the middle of the "too big to fail" debate.

The Politics of Banking and Too Big to Fail

Aaron Burr and Alexander Hamilton were not the last two people ever argue over the politics and merits of banking and its implications on "customers, communities, or the economy in general." When Capital One announced its proposed acquisition of ING Direct USA in June 2011, political enemies and critics came out against the move in full-force. US Representative for Massachusetts Barney Frank asked the Federal Reserve to "deepen its review of Capital One Financial's proposed $9 billion acquisition of ING Direct USA."[32] In a letter sent to Ben Bernanke, the then chairman of the Federal Reserve, Frank requested the Fed to hold public hearings to "explore the impact of this acquisition on consumers, communities, and the economy in general." In addition to public hearings, Mr. Frank asked that the Fed grant the public at least "60 days" to weigh in on the acquisition.

Frank's reason for the inquiry was that he believed the proposed purchase "would create the fifth-largest bank in the United States. For this reason alone, care should be taken to thoroughly examine the impact of this purchase with respect to the consolidation of banking assets, the provision of credit by the resulting bank and compliance with the Community Reinvestment Act." In addition, Frank was concerned at the number of acquisitions Capital One had already made in previous years.

The letter also raised questions about Capital One's dealmaking record, saying that consumer advocacy groups have issued concerns about its past acquisitions. In a statement in support of Frank, John Taylor, president of the National Community Reinvestment Coalition, wondered, "We already have four too-big-to-fail banks, why make a fifth?"[33]

In an interview with the *New York Times* at the time, Tatiana Stead, spokeswoman for Capital One, called the concerns "baseless" and cited that the acquisition "further reduces, rather than increases, our overall risk profile."[34]

Capital One responded officially by sending a letter to the Fed bank based in Virginia arguing that there was no need for a further extension or comment period and that the public had ample time to express concerns since the announcement in June of that year. It further argued, "Capital One's proven record of meeting the needs of the communities it serves is evidenced by the Community Reinvestment Act ('CRA') performance records of its subsidiary banks, Capital One Bank (USA), National Association ('COBNA') and Capital One, National Association ('CONA'). As noted in the Notice, the banks' primary federal supervisors rated the CRA performance of COBNA as 'Outstanding' and CONA as 'Satisfactory' at their most recent CRA performance evaluations. In addition, ING Bank's CRA performance was rated 'Outstanding' at its last evaluation by the Office of Thrift Supervision ('OTS')."[35] Capital One also argued that it had implemented what it deemed "robust compliance risk management systems to ensure compliance with fair lending and other consumer protection laws." It also cited benefits to consumers, namely access to a much broader array of deposit and loan products that ING Bank does not currently offer, including fixed-rate home mortgage loans, and a broad network of automated teller machines ("ATMs"). In the end, the Fed agreed with Capital One and they were free to acquire ING Direct.

By February 2012, Capital One officially announced that it completed its acquisition of the ING Direct business in the United States from the ING Group for $6.3 billion and approximately 54 million Capital One shares, representing 9.7 ownership stake. Headquartered in Wilmington, DE, ING Direct was the largest direct bank in the country at the time and was dedicated to "inspiring Americans to become a nation of savers."[36] For his part, Fairbank was pleased with how things panned out. They were a bank in the mortgage game, this time on solid ground. The news blew over, and Capital One was able to finalize the purchase. In a press release, Fairbank, rather uncharacteristically, gave a long and strongly worded defense for the purchase of ING Direct to allay all fears that consumers may have developed with Frank's inquiry: "We expect the ING Direct acquisition will deliver compelling financial results in the near-term, and enhance our ability to deliver sustained value over the long-term to our customers, our communities, and our shareholders. Capital One has great national scale lending businesses, local banking scale in attractive markets, a powerful national brand, proven analytical capabilities, and tens of millions of customer relationships. ING Direct brings the leading direct banking franchise in the nation, over seven million loyal customers who are early digital adopters, and national reach in banking with proven digital capabilities. Together, we are well-positioned to create an institution at the forefront of where banking is going, and to continue to deliver strong and sustainable shareholder value through a combination of superior returns, growth potential, and strong capital generation."[37]

The Accolades

In addition to acquiring ING Direct and officially moving into the D2C banking market, Capital One enjoyed other successes in 2012. It was recognized by J.D. Power and Associates for Outstanding Customer Service[38] and it was also named by *Fortune* Magazine as one of the "100 Best Companies to Work for." In the same year, it was recognized as One of America's Top 50 Community-Minded Companies by The Civic 50 survey, the first comprehensive ranking of S&P 500 corporations that best use their time, talent, and resources to improve the quality of life in the communities where they do business. The survey was conducted by the National Conference on Citizenship (NCoC) and Points of Light, the nation's definitive experts on civic engagement, in partnership with Bloomberg LP.[39] Capital One weathered the storms and came out of the startup world and launched into full-fledged Big-Bankdom with aplomb.

And what's truly remarkable is when every other bank was floundering, Capital One was maximizing opportunities, seeing holes in the market, and working strategically, rather than combatively, to seek agencies' and the consumers' approval. They did so at a remarkable rate. While it could have been a time for Fairbank to step back and take a break, after riding out a tsunami of an economic downtown, Fairbank was far from ending the game. He was in double overtime, and he no plans of skating off the ice anytime soon. In fact, once again not discouraged by the opposition or naysayers, Fairbank had some more ideas he wanted to test and run by consumers—not just digital banking, banking on the cloud.

"Digital isn't a channel.
It's a way of life."

—RICHARD FAIRBANK

CHAPTER FOUR

CHANGING TECHNOLOGY

Innovative Banking Solutions

I n the middle of the night on a German highway in December 2012, banking as we all know it changed. A little-known entrepreneur and owner of a Dutch FinTech start-up, Ohpen, was in the final stages of cutting the deal of his life. Chris Zadeh and his wife were on their way to their Christmas holiday in Zermatt, Switzerland, when he received the call from Amazon in Seattle. *The contract was almost approved. He was so close. He had to seal this deal. If the contract fell through, he would lose his company, millions of euros, not to mention the past three years of his life that he dedicated to building a core-engine bank that sits on the cloud.* The only thing standing in his way were all the parties involved, namely Amazon Web Services (AWS) that hosted the cloud, Robeco, Zadeh's banking client who wanted to use his services, and the Dutch National Bank, which made sure all Dutch banks and their vendors (like Ohpen) complied with EU banking regulations.

As it does with all banks, the Dutch National Bank had the right to audit Robeco, which meant it could also audit its vendors—like Ohpen, a FinTech software company that provided the core-engine banking software for Robeco. Since Ohpen used a cloud-based service—AWS—to host its software, that would mean that the DNB would also need to be able to audit AWS. If Zadeh wanted to finalize his contract with the first bank ever to sit on the cloud, the Dutch National Bank had to approve Zadeh's company's use of AWS as a "material subcontractor." However, this would mean that AWS would have to change their original contract language to include the "Right to Audit." This was ultimately opening Pandora's box for AWS. It would mean that an outside entity could essentially audit or gain access to information on their cloud servers.

This was a highly complex, intricate, and sensitive issue. If AWS didn't allow this right to audit, then the DNB wouldn't approve Robeco sitting on the AWS cloud. But of course AWS's major concern was that they didn't want *any of its clients' rights being violated or having prying eyes on their intellectual properties.* For months Zadeh wrangled with several members and lawyers from all parties. His priority was to get AWS to change this standard contract language to allow the Dutch National Bank to do an audit at the Amazon servers. "If we couldn't get that done, there would be no cloud banking, because the Central Banks in Europe would have stopped it," Zadeh says.[1] This was an enormous undertaking.

Zadeh was an unknown entity at the time, especially in the eyes of a giant powerhouse like Amazon. Nevertheless, he reached out to the chief technology officer of Amazon, who happened to be Dutch—Werner Vogels. Zadeh knew what was on the line for Amazon and told him as much: "If you want the financial services market, you will have to arrange this. I know we are a little company in your eyes, and if you're Amazon, you are more interested in getting Bank of America on the cloud. But whoever you're going to sign, every regulator in the world will want this audit right. If you don't have this audit right, you will not get one financial regulated company." Throughout the night Zadeh stayed on the phone while he drove, all the while working through the final stages of the contract with his colleague, Lydia van de Voort, who had left a Christmas party back in Amsterdam, jumped on a bicycle in the frigid temperatures, and rode over to the Ohpen offices to go through the contract over the phone line by line. By sun up, the deal was done. All parties approved. For the first time ever, a bank was going to sit on the cloud—more accurately the AWS servers. Cloud banking was now a reality.

What exactly does that mean? Though misunderstood, the cloud is not that difficult to explain. The cloud is not a physical thing, but rather a virtual thing that relies on a vast network of remote servers around the globe. These servers are connected and meant to operate as a single system in order to store and manage data, run applications, or deliver content or a service. Most of us use the cloud every day to stream our favorite Netflix shows, play Minecraft, access our email, and check our Instagram. Instead of accessing our data or files from a personal computer or from a network of servers on-premises, when in the cloud, we are able to access them online from any internet-capable device—our phones, our laptops, and iPads. The information is available anywhere, anytime.

Just for some perspective in 2008, most people were just hearing about the "cloud" and no one, let alone banks, thought of processing and storing one's financial data there. Up until 2012, no bank had operated with production data or applications in the cloud before. Rather, every single bank in the world built their own platform, or what is known as a legacy system, within their own buildings. Zadeh argued this was wildly inefficient, "The [banks] purchased or built software and then hired their own developers, application managers, and systems engineers to build, change, patch, and maintain it. They stored all their company's information in one location in giant computers in their own data center. Each bank essentially reinvented the wheel every time they set up their banking systems." The results? Usually massive issues, amounts of time wasted, work forces required, and expenses. The process to integrate or migrate customers onto new platforms was costly and usually a logistical nightmare. He believed cloud-technology would reduce and minimize these expenses. Fairbank, though he didn't know and has never met Zadeh, agreed.

Digitizing Banking

Meanwhile back in Virginia, Capital One was focusing on their new integration of ING Direct. And just two months after Amazon and Ohpen cut their deal, on February 1, 2013, Capital One announced the launching of their Direct Banking brand—Capital One 360, which was the rebranded ING Direct. They adopted more than 3,000 customer touch points from the bank. Their main issue, of course, was not just rebranding, but infrastructure. In addition to acquiring ING Direct, they had acquired HSBC's US credit card business. Fairbank explained in the 2013 Annual Report, "The big focus of the HSBC US credit card business integration has been to disentangle the systems and operations of that business from the parent company and integrate them with Capital One's infrastructure." Integrating banks and migrating customer information onto one core-engine platform that served all the banks required what Fairbank called "deep industry specialization." But he argued, "We're well positioned at the forefront of where banking is going over the last two decades, we have transformed our company and positioned ourselves to compete effectively and deliver sustained value as the financial services industry evolves."[2]

The acquisitions they completed in 2012 were important to this transformation, because, he explained, they gave them "core deposits, national banking reach, access to assets, and enhanced digital and customer capabilities that will help us compete successfully for years to come." Fairbank was well aware that the financial services landscape was evolving at an accelerated pace. Direct banking, mobile banking, and banking on the cloud were just some of those landscapes. "Understanding where the world is going and positioning ourselves relative to end-game success will continue to be a critical management focus," Fairbank added.

National Consolidation

In addition to changing infrastructures and the way banking was done, national consolidation continued to shape the financial services industry as well. Fairbank had predicted for years (in his long personally written annual report letters), that the earliest phases of national consolidation began "not one company at a time, but one product at a time." He stated credit cards, auto finance, and online brokerage all were stripped away from traditional banks by national players with increasing scale advantages. He further predicted that products and businesses that were now highly consolidated were essentially off-limits to local and regional players without national scale.

This is where he saw the opportunity: Traditional deposit banking had been slower to consolidate nationally, but he knew that the trend toward national scale was "inexorable." Direct banking on a national scale was, in his mind, inevitable. "We have a large, national customer base, including the 7.5 million passionate 'early digital adopters' who came with the ING Direct acquisition," he wrote. Since most people have grown accustomed to mobile banking, it's hard to remember that, in 2012, most people were still making deposits at banks or through ATMs. The idea of digitally transferring money from one account to another, let alone one person to another still wasn't "a thing" in 2012–2013.

But, in 2013, Capital One had the nation's largest internet bank. That being said, Fairbank wasn't ready to turn his back on local traditional deposit banking and commercial banking. "We have strong local positions in these businesses, including branches in attractive local markets, and a well-established and successful commercial banking business focused on primary banking relationships," Fairbank continued modestly.

> **❝ But, in 2013, Capital One had the nation's largest internet bank. That being said, Fairbank wasn't ready to turn his back on local traditional deposit banking and commercial banking.**

Needless to say, Fairbank saw where the future was headed and it was in digital banking. He also knew with that change the company and its talent recruitment had to adapt this change as well. "Digital banking has given us a powerful associate recruiting platform, and we are attracting first-rate digital talent, including many people from outside of banking, all with deep fluency in digital technology," Fairbank explained.[3] With this new talent, they began to focus on customer-facing features, which primarily meant apps and design elements, including new designs for online bill payment. They also rolled out mobile deals and new apps, like the "Purchase Eraser," which allowed customers to use their rewards to "erase" their previous purchases via their mobile app. They also continued to focus on driving digital innovation.

In 2012, their Digital Lab was selected from among over 50 nominees for the inaugural Cognizant/Corporate Executive Board Award for Innovation in Financial Services. Fairbank hoped all these calculated moves positioned Capital One "to be a leader in the digital transformation of banking."[4]

Positioning Capital One as a "Digital Leader Technology" changed everything they do. Fairbank argued it was changing the way "they work, learn, communicate, and live." He was well aware that entire industries had been invented or disrupted by software and the power of the digital revolution. From the beginning, Fairbank knew that banking was inherently a digital product. As the CIO Robert Alexander said at the beginning of this book, "Our products are just ephemeral products. It is principally software and data." Though Capital One had been on the digital scene from the beginning, Fairbank acknowledged momentum around digital was building across financial services. They weren't the lone players. Other banks were catching up and, on top of that, consumer demand required they all do so. "The staggering rate of adoption of smartphones and the proliferation of technology is rapidly and dramatically changing consumer behavior," Fairbank acknowledged.[5] Consumers were coming to expect what he deemed "rich digital experiences" from all companies—banks included. And he noticed, software was the predominant way consumers interacted with their banks, and that engagement will only increase. The writing was on the wall: there was a lot of competition out there and it wasn't just from banks, but rather, these "FinTech" software companies who were coming up with new and better ways to pay for things—or what is called in the industry as the "payment space."

> **❝ Our products are just ephemeral products. It is principally software and data."**

With the payment and software spaces and competition broadening, the ability to efficiently store and use vast amounts of data was something Capital One could leverage. Fairbank believed that "Ultimately, the winners in banking will have the mindset of a world-class software and information company and the scale and capabilities of a diversified bank. To succeed in a digital world, a company can't just bolt digital capabilities onto the side of a fundamentally analog business."[6] In other words, simply transferring "brick-and-mortar activities to online and mobile platforms," was just scratching the surface. If that is all a bank did, it was missing out on the opportunity for new, virtual experiences. "Digital isn't a channel. It's a way of life," Fairbank said. "At Capital One, we are deeply embedding technology, data, design, and software development into how we work. Most of the leverage and most of our focus is in establishing the foundational underpinnings of a great digital company."[7]

Preparing a Workforce for the Digital Age

"Building a technology-driven bank starts with talent" is something Fairbank has reiterated from the beginning of Capital One. But by 2013 they began to invest more in training and development of their talent and building up their workspaces in what Fairbank termed "talent-dense locations" that rival those of leading technology firms—including San Francisco, Manhattan, Chicago, Plano, and Washington, DC. They also began to hire even more engineers, product managers, designers, and data scientists—some of whom worked outside of banking. Fairbank did this, he said, to "challenge how conventional banking works." Sounding every bit like a FinTech, startup-entrepreneur, Fairbank said, "We're using iterative software development methods and modern architecture to accelerate innovation. We're streamlining our core systems and applications to enable faster deployment. The use of open-source and cloud technology is expanding across the company. And we are re-inventing our internal processes, operations, and governance to ensure that we have the agility to get to market quickly and securely."[8] This was the first mention of Capital One investigating and using the cloud.

It wasn't just about the infrastructure. They also recognized they couldn't sacrifice great design for the sake of scalability or functionality. Consumers still wanted simple, intuitive, and easy-use applications. Again, they turned to hiring talent to make sure they were doing their best to keep consumers happy. They hired leading designers from prominent technology firms and leading educational institutions, including Stanford's design school. They adopted "design thinking" principles that emphasized the User Experience (UX). Design thinking is a method of design that empathizes with customers, then rapidly develops and deploys prototypes, in order to test new ideas.

Capital One built several on the premise "usability labs" to enable them to explore in real time "what delights or frustrates customers" and then to respond quickly to those insights. In 2014, Capital One acquired Adaptive Path, a legendary San Francisco-based pioneer in UX design and orchestrating end-to-end service experiences.

> **"** Digital isn't a channel. It's a way of life," Fairbank said. "At Capital One, we are deeply embedding technology, data, design, and software development into how we work. Most of the leverage and most of our focus is in establishing the foundational underpinnings of a great digital company."

Moving into the Payment Space

In 2014, they continued to focus on delivering digital products and services to customers. With the launch of Capital One 360, they offered a simple digital experience, but they continued to expand their offerings and to develop new features. In 2014, they began partnering with Apple. They were one of only a handful of banks to be included in the launch of Apple Pay™. In the same year they also introduced Capital One Wallet, a mobile payment app that synced with Apple Pay and enabled customers to make purchases, view balances, track spending, and receive real-time notifications of charges and alerts. In addition to this app, customers also were able to use the Capital One Credit Tracker, a free online and mobile tool that provided customers with access to their credit scores, as well as simulators that demonstrate how to use credit wisely and improve scores, which was an extension of their extended and exerted effort to educate their customers. They also debuted Second Look, a free service that automatically scanned for duplicate or unusual charges and alerted customers when they occurred.

Leveraging Social Media and Customer Engagement

Like most companies expanding in the digital space, advertising and being present on social media channels was a key way Capital One continued to deliver their message. As a longtime successful advertiser and visible brand, especially on television, Capital One expanded their social media advertising and search engine marketing. They used social media for many of the same purposes most companies do—to drive traffic and new business—but also for recruitment, philanthropy, as well as customer service. They even went so far as to release a handle to @AskCapitalOne to offer real-time conversations and responses.

Using Technology to Enhance the Mission

"We are a mission-driven company focused on serving our customers. We measure our success by their success," Fairbank said.[9] Though Fairbank believed that and spent his career trying to build a company that he felt empowered customers, he was still confronted with criticism and naysayers. He understood why. He knew that many banks lost focus on the customers they served and were looking out for their bottom line alone (or to line their own pockets). The Great Recession, numerous banking scandals, Ponzi schemes, and the "Too Big to Fail" debates only exacerbated an already skeptical public's derision of banks. "Sadly, a lot of people feel that banks are motivated by what's best for themselves, not their customers," Fairbank acknowledged.[10] He believed his bank was different and felt strongly that his ultimate goal was to help customers succeed.

Fairbank founded the company on the ideas of democratizing the credit process and helping customers save money. He was well aware that his company made money on interest paid, but he also felt that he wasn't so desperate to make a profit that he would compromise the financial health of his customers. For him that meant helping people use credit wisely. "We strive to help our customers follow four important principles: get a clear and fair deal; don't borrow more than you should; pay on time; and pay down."[11] He knew helping people use credit wisely sometimes meant leaving potential profits behind, but he added, it was an "easy choice" for him. "It's the right thing to do for our customers, and it's how we are building an enduring customer franchise," Fairbank added.

With National Access Comes National Visibility and Commitment to Philanthropy

Despite some public criticism for being now one of the "Big Banks," as they neared twenty-five years of being in business, Capital One was enjoying the fact that they were one of the most recognized brands, not just in banking but in American culture as well. They had campaigns featuring fan favorites like Jimmy Fallon and Alec Baldwin (though the Visigoths still enjoyed national play too). They were virtually everywhere. They sponsored the Capital One Bowl (for twelve years running) and in 2012 they were the corporate sponsor of the NCAA Final Four. Besides marketing and advertising campaigns, they made concerted efforts to be active within communities and focused on volunteering efforts. In 2012, Capital One associates volunteered more than 260,000 hours to mentor small business owners, counsel first-time homebuyers, and teach the basics of personal money management. Associates from Legal, Finance, IT, and other specialized areas provided nonprofits with almost 6,000 hours of pro bono services in 2012.[12]

> In 2012, Capital One associates volunteered more than 260,000 hours to mentor small business owners, counsel first-time homebuyers, and teach the basics of personal money management. Associates from Legal, Finance, IT, and other specialized areas provided nonprofits with almost 6,000 hours of pro bono services in 2012.

Though criticized for their lack of philanthropic commitment during the ING Direct merger,[13] Capital One reported that they made more than $45 million in philanthropic grants during the 2012 year and provided more than $1.3 billion in loans and investments, which they argued helped to create "9,200 safe and affordable places to live and more than 10,000 jobs in the communities we call home."[14] In the days following Superstorm Sandy, Capital One made $1.5 million in grants to local and national nonprofits for their recovery efforts. They also promised $3 million to a New York City program that would make interest-free loans to nonprofits that suffered property damage and other storm-related losses. In addition to their continued efforts to support national programs that benefited veterans and military spouses, they set out to hire veterans themselves. In 2012 Capital One hired almost 500 veterans, and committed $4.5 million over the following three years to the US Chamber of Commerce Hiring Our Heroes initiative. And they also committed to a three-year, $800,000 investment in Count Me In for Women's Economic Independence, which mentored small business owners who are veterans, spouses, or domestic partners of veterans.[15] Keenly aware that despite what seemed like rampant phone use, many people still didn't have access to the digital world due to what Fairbank said were "gaps in education, skills, and financial resources." In an effort to bridge this gap, he pledged that Capital One would invest $150 million in community grants and initiatives. His hope was ultimately to train people for the jobs of today and tomorrow by 2019.

As Capital One approached its twentieth year in business it was on the cusp of the rapidly changing banking market, but as always it was prepared. Taking advantage of advances in FinTech, core banking, D2C, retail customer apps, and moving away from legacy systems and beginning exploration options like the cloud, they were more prepared than ever to expand. But, they were also proving they were here to stay. They were ready to put down roots.

"My most important job as CEO has been to attract great people and then to create an environment where they can be great."

—RICHARD FAIRBANK

CHAPTER FIVE

CAPITAL ONE TODAY

*Lessons Learned and
Building with the Future in Mind*

The years between 2014–2018 were a time of accelerated growth. There was a definitive need to create a space for the growing company. In 2014, construction crews broke ground on the brand-new headquarters in McLean, Virginia. By the time it was completed in 2018, it had become the second tallest building in Virginia (surpassed only by the historic Washington Monument, of course). However, though it was a mammoth 940,500 square foot structure designed by HKS and CallisonRTKL architecture firms, it still "came up short" to meet the demands of their growing company.[1] Upon completion, there was not enough office space to accommodate the growing staff. Nevertheless, for those it could accommodate it included full-size basketball courts, FedEx, a PowerUp tech bar, outdoor terraces, a massive food court, performing arts center, and even had plans for a grocery (Wegmans). The building and campus were designed to help "foster collaboration and inclusion" and included spaces like "touchdown space" where employees could get away from their own work stations in order to meet face-to-face. With the hope of breaking down "perceived barriers" and to give the feeling of transparency, the floors are all interconnected by sets of zipper stairs.

Most of the space was designed with change, growth, and flexibility in mind. Many of the rooms were created to be multifunctional or expandable. Since Capital One has always seen themselves as very much a part of the "community" it was no surprise they worked with the local community to build a public sky park, which featured a beer garden, dog park, water features, a playground, pickle ball courts, game plaza, bocce courts, and much more. In addition to it being state of the art office space, it achieved carbon neutrality on direct greenhouse gas emissions. All the new office construction and large renovations were certified LEED Silver or higher, while the new corporate headquarters in McLean, Virginia, was certified LEED Gold in 2019.

 In 2018, the seeds of our investments bore fruit." That fruit was $28.1 billion and record earnings per share (EPS) of $11.82.

Building Beyond the Four Walls— From the Inside Out

In a letter to shareholders and friends in 2019, Fairbank stated, "It's an extraordinary time to be at Capital One." Citing record revenues and profits, Fairbank added, "Our financial results in 2018 were rooted in years of previous choices about growth, investments, and risk management. Those choices often resulted in near-term costs, but they also planted the seeds of future growth and financial returns. In 2018, the seeds of our investments bore fruit." That fruit was $28.1 billion and record earnings per share (EPS) of $11.82. Fairbank attributed Capital One's "investments in products, technology, brand, and resilience" to their growth. On the cusp of their twenty-fifth anniversary as a public company, Fairbank was in a celebratory mood—he had every right to be. He was seeing his vision become reality and reminded shareholders of that vision:

> We were founded on the belief that the banking industry would be revolutionized by information and technology, beginning with credit cards. Back then, credit cards were a one size-fits-all business that relied on judgmental decision-making by underwriters and marketers. . . . We set out to turn one-size-fits-all into "mass customization," delivering the right product to the right customer at the right time and at the right price. We believed that by de-averaging the market, we could smash the price of credit and also democratize it. Our vision wasn't just about credit cards. We thought that credit cards would be the first banking product to be transformed because they were direct-marketed, national in scope, and there was great financial leverage in getting marketing and credit risk decisions right. We believed that if we created a company with these capabilities, we would be positioned at the forefront of the digital revolution that would ultimately sweep across all of the banking industry. Our rallying cry was, "Build a technology

company that does banking, and compete against banks that use technology."[2]

Building the Original FinTech

Fairbank had every right to assert, as he did, that "Capital One was the original "FinTech," (though FinTech wasn't even a term when they got started). In the letter he argued it wasn't always easy, "We had more passion than customers and more belief than believers." He reminisced about his early days leading a startup, facing so many of the same obstacles that entrepreneurs face today: "recruiting talent, building modern technology from scratch, conducting tests, and incubating results." He admitted that while the initial idea came quickly, it took "five lonely years" until he tasted any success. At the twenty-five years' point, he could finally proudly assert that Capital One indeed was "one of the nation's largest credit card businesses."

They were also international—expanding in the United Kingdom and Canada. Though only venturing into retail banking just 15 years ago, Capital One was the nation's fifth-largest consumer bank and eighth-largest bank overall.[3]

Addressing the economic crisis, which he called the Great Recession, coupled with the digital revolution, Fairbank pointed out that entire industries disappeared and new ones appeared. But as the digital revolution accelerated, and some industries and banks panicked, Capital One "cheered." Fairbank knew all along that Capital One was built to capitalize on the changing industry structure. "That's who we are," Fairbank asserted. While most industries were still floundering in 2012 and reeling from the recession, Capital One was engaging in acquisitions. They also saw themselves very much the outsiders.

"To see the future of banking," Fairbank wrote, "we didn't look at how banking worked or what other banks were doing. We looked instead at how technology was changing our lives. We reveled in the miracle that Google could find any information, anywhere in the world, in a fraction of a second. We saw how Waze could instantly find the fastest route and immediately adapt it if traffic changed. And we marveled at how Netflix could somehow find a movie you love, even though you had never heard of it and weren't looking for it in the first place." What all the companies shared with Capital One was, Fairbank believed, they were "real-time and intelligent." In other words, they offered instant solutions, customized for customers, anywhere in the world at any time.

" What all the companies shared with Capital One was, Fairbank believed, they were "real-time and intelligent." In other words, they offered instant solutions, customized for customers, anywhere in the world at any time.

Building a "Real-Time and Intelligent" Bank

As customers began to acclimate and expect "real-time and intelligent" offerings in every aspect of their lives, they would also expect banking to follow suit. But, Fairbank said, "banks aren't built to deliver real-time and intelligent solutions. In fact, they are built for just the opposite. They are built on legacy technology optimized for batch processing. They employ complex, manual processes that operate in organizational silos. And many have corporate cultures that are resistant to change." He admitted, that despite all their technological advances, know-how, and talent, "even Capital One, which two decades before had been designed around technology and information, was not designed for a world that was rapidly moving to real-time and intelligent solutions."

Fairbank could see the puck was on the move. Once again he planned for it. In 2012, while the economic crisis was turning a corner, and they were busy acquiring, they were also rebuilding their own bank from what he called, "the bottom of the tech stack up." Despite that Capital One had already done that twenty years prior, the world had changed so much that Capital One, and "pretty much all of corporate America" he argued, had been stranded with "insufficient tech talent and antiquated foundational technology, data ecosystems, and methods of working." He further explained that up until then the usual method employed to adapt to change in corporate America was to "work forward from where you are rather than backward from what technology enables." This, he argued, leads to subpar technology that is simply "digitizing analog activities or building customer-facing apps on top of outdated infrastructure." He argued that most companies are simply "bolting new technology capabilities onto legacy operations or trying to quarantine their modern technology and innovation to select pockets of the organization." This, he knew, wasn't going to yield results and it wasn't going to give Capital One a competitive advantage in the years to come. What he needed was to rethink how banking works entirely and build technology that does banking. Capital One went "all in."

Building the Talent and Processes

For years, Capital One had been what they considered a leading technology company that banked. In other words, they worked primarily in software and data. Instead of hiring a stable of financiers, Capital One focused on building a tech-capable company. By 2018, 85 percent of their technology workforce were engineers. Capital One embraced advanced technology strategies and modern data environments.

Like so many software and FinTech companies, Capital One adopted agile management practices, and not just for software delivery. Though common lingo inside software companies, most are unfamiliar with the term *agile management,* which at its most rudimentary is a project management style that favors individuals and interactions over processes and tools. It focuses more on working software than documentation (aka bureaucracy), customer collaboration over contract negotiation, and responding to a change over following a strict plan. It is primarily an iterative approach to planning project processes. That means the project is completed in small sections or iterations. Then each section or iteration is reviewed and critiqued by the project team, which should include representatives of the project's various stakeholders.

All of the insights gained from the review or critique process are then used to determine what the next steps should be in the project. The primary benefit of working with agile project management style is the ability to respond to issues—in real-time and intelligently—as they arise throughout the course of the project. In Capital One, it wasn't just the software teams adopting this approach. They deployed it across the board, and even Legal and Audit were using a version of this to get work done. In addition to agile management, Capital One adopted a DevOps culture—also common nomenclature in the startup and FinTech worlds. DevOps comes the "You Built It, You Own It" mindset, but what it really means is that it is a set of software development processes (Dev) and information-technology operations (Ops) that are combined to shorten and enhance the development of systems. It's designed to quickly deliver features, fixes, and updates, and requires that teams work collaboratively from beginning to end. Though they were by every means a large corporation, they were operating every bit like a small software startup.

Building on the Cloud: Advantages and Risks

By 2018, the vast majority of Capital One's operating and customer-facing applications operated in the cloud, which allowed Capital One associates to design real-time, intelligent experiences. Which means Capital One could monitor, access, and develop in real time, and with a cloud-based server that was infinitely scalable. With AWS there was no limit to the amount of data Capital One could store. Not all clouds are equal. Capital One sits on what is considered one of the best and safest cloud servers in the world—the Amazon Web Services (AWS) cloud. That means as a vendor, AWS is responsible for keeping the data that Capital One has stored on the cloud safe. There are several protocols and alerts in place to maintain the safety and security of a client's data, however, there is no 100 percent safeguard, especially when humans are involved.

On July 29, 2019, Capital One released a statement that said they had discovered a security breach, though Capital One refers to it as an "incident." An "unauthorized access" had occurred on July 19, 2019. Capital One was notified about the breach by AWS monitoring system. In the statement, Capital One admitted that the unauthorized access had compromised the data of 106 million people in both the US and Canada. As soon as they were made aware Capital One notified the FBI. Shortly after, Capital One was notified by the FBI that a previous employee and software engineer for Amazon Web Services was responsible for the hack.

For their part, Amazon stated that the hacker's employment at their company had nothing to do with the hack. Though she was once an employee at AWS, her employment had ended in 2016. According to Amazon, "She used an entrance point that was a misconfiguration of a Capital One designed web application and not the underlying Amazon-designed cloud-based infrastructure."[4] Amazon Web Services further said, "AWS was not compromised in any way and functioned as it was designed."[5]

As soon as the news broke, panic ensued all over the world that millions of customers' personal data was compromised. Immediately, people were enraged and blamed the cloud—or Amazon. Though Amazon claimed its cloud was secure and that the former employee used a hacking technique that Amazon argued could have been used by anyone (at least any hacker), this news did not bring comfort, especially to those that were hacked. It simply solidified, in some customers' minds, that their personal information being stored with credit card companies is too vulnerable. Furthermore, customers were angry that it took two weeks for Capital One to notify them. Several Capital One customers took to Twitter to air their grievances, "I have a capital one credit card, I learned of the hack from The Washington Post, @CapitalOne ain't sent me an apology email YET" or "Is Capital One leaving its customers in the dark? Or is wait of this length or longer normal when it comes to notifying customers of a hack?"

In the US, there are no federal laws requiring banks or other businesses who store their customer's data digitally to inform people of hacks, though most states do have laws in keeping with California's 2002 law that states "notifications must be made in the most expedient time possible without unreasonable delay and consistent with law enforcement needs."[6]

In the July 29, 2019 press release, Fairbank argued that, "The speed with which we were able to diagnose and fix this vulnerability, and determine its impact, was enabled by our cloud operating model." But he did not explain why it took so long to notify the public, who could have immediately changed passwords, monitored their accounts, and protected their information if they were immediately notified.

Fairbank admitted Capital One's failure and promised to make amends, stating, "While I am grateful that the perpetrator has been caught, I am deeply sorry for what has happened. I sincerely apologize for the understandable worry this incident must be causing those affected and I am committed to making it right." Fairbank assured customers that no credit card account numbers or log-in credentials were compromised and over 99 percent of Social Security numbers were not compromised at all. He further explained that the largest category of information accessed was information on consumers and small businesses as of the time they applied for Capital One credit card products from 2005 through early 2019. This information included personal information Capital One routinely collects at the time it receives credit card applications, including names, addresses, zip codes/postal codes, phone numbers, email addresses, dates of birth, and self-reported income. Beyond the credit card application data, the individual also obtained portions of credit card customer data, including: Customer status data, e.g., credit scores, credit limits, balances, payment history, contact information, and fragments of transaction data from a total of 23 days during 2016, 2017, and 2018.

After the Data Breach

Capital One took steps to notify those affected through a variety of channels and offered free credit monitoring and identity protection for all those affected. Fairbank wrote, "Safeguarding our customers' information is essential to our mission and our role as a financial institution. We have invested heavily in cybersecurity and will continue to do so. We will incorporate the learnings from this incident to further strengthen our cyber defenses."

While securing customers' data is top priority, Fairbank and Capital One had to assure shareholders that there were not significant financial impacts. Fairbank asserted, "We expect the incident to generate incremental costs of approximately $100 to $150 million in 2019. Expected costs are largely driven by customer notifications, credit monitoring, technology costs, and legal support. We expect to accrue the costs for customer notification and credit monitoring in 2019. The expected incremental costs related to the incident will be separately reported as an adjusting item as it relates to the Company's financial results." Finally, Fairbank concluded that they had already been investing heavily in cyber security and that the company would continue to do so. Of course, the company carried insurance to cover the cost of such related incidents and the press release stated they paid a 10-million-dollar deductible and the insurance coverage limit is $400 million.[7]

> Though a temporary blow to the company, and a wake-up call for all corporate entities with client data, the breach did show that the AWS cloud was and is safe, in fact it was the reason they were alerted of the breach in the first place.

No one quite knows why the former Amazon employee targeted Capital One. According to news reports, she seemed to be having serious emotional issues and had trouble maintaining employment. (As of this writing, the investigation is still ongoing.) What we do know is that she didn't only target Capital One; she had attempted to hack into several corporate databases to steal user information. She never accessed the bank accounts or sold the data, however. She did post the stolen Capital One files on GitHub, a website developers use to share programming code. As soon as Capital One was made aware they fixed the configuration vulnerability that the former Amazon employee exploited and promptly began working with federal law enforcement.

Though a temporary blow to the company, and a wake-up call for all corporate entities with client data, the breach did show that the AWS cloud was and is safe, in fact it was the reason they were alerted of the breach in the first place. It also showed that Fairbank and Capital One were willing to admit failures and make things right—always—for their customers and made them reinforce their technology efforts.

Building Modern Digital Tools to Create Better Customer Experiences

During this period of expansion and being on the cloud, Capital One also had successes, specifically with their online and mobile customer services platform. In both 2017 and 2018, Capital One was awarded the J.D. Power award for the "Highest in Overall US Banking App Satisfaction." In addition to their mobile banking app, they focused intensely on other customer service features as well. In line with their long history of teaching consumers about their own financial health, Capital One launched CreditWise®, a free app available to everyone—not just Capital One customers. It was designed to help consumers monitor their credit, while also giving customers the tools they would need to understand and improve their credit score. It also protected customers from identity theft and fraud, and helped monitor transactions so customers could make quick decisions and understand their spending habits—and even mishaps, such as double payments, sudden increases in spending, sudden jumps in bills, accidental tips, or odd purchases. With real-time purchase notifications every time the card is used, customers could be proactive in the protection of their financial health and identity. If there was suspicious activity, Capital One could instantly lock the card.[8]

Building the Capital One Cafés

By 2019, virtually every banking service Capital One offered was available digitally online or in an app. From any computer or smartphone, a customer could open a Capital One checking or savings account in five minutes. However, Capital One still felt that a physical presence was important too. They knew that what customers expected in that presence has changed dramatically over the past few years. Their answer to having a physical presence was what Fairbank announced as Capital One Cafés. Think less "branch office" and more "showroom." Located in what Fairbank called "iconic urban locations," these cafés offer "experiences." A customer or potential customer (you don't have to be a Capital One customer to enter the café) can come in, grab a cup of Peet's Coffee, enjoy some free WiFi, sample some of Capital One's products or technology, or even talk to a Capital One Money Coach. In addition to the cafés, Capital One still offers more traditional branches for various customer service needs and more complex transactions.

Building More Relationships

In July 2018, Capital One announced a long-term agreement to be the exclusive issuer of co-branded and private-label credit cards for Walmart, the world's largest retailer. Then in January 2019, they announced an agreement to acquire approximately $9 billion of existing Walmart credit card loans at a favorable price and terms. Fairbank said, "We're eager to work with Walmart to deliver amazing value, deepen customer relationships, and use technology and digital innovation to create exceptional experiences for customers across America."[9] Capital One had spent many years building and expanding relationships, and it looks as though they are continuing to do so.

Building a Brand for the Future

Capital One has always been known—even from their earliest years—as a brand to watch. In 2018, they spent $2.2 billion on marketing and advertising, virtually unmatched in the industry. Fairbank attributes this investment for reasons that he said, "drove solid customer and deposit growth in the retail bank, strong credit card account growth, and 15 percent growth in domestic card purchase volume." In 2018, they introduced a new card, Savor®, a unique credit card that pays 4 percent unlimited rewards on dining and entertainment. At the same time, Capital One launched its "Banking Reimagined" advertising campaign, which publicized their digital banking tools and the Capital One Café experience. Iconic and well-known celebrities—Jennifer Garner and Samuel L. Jackson—touted the merits of Venture® and Quicksilver® cards, and were virtually ubiquitous on television sets. They also continued to sponsor the Capital One Arena in what they considered their "hometown of Washington, DC" (McLean is a suburb of the Nation's Capital). In the 2018, Capitals' run to the Stanley Cup, Capital One enjoyed both local and national exposure during what Fairbank called "months of late-night (and nail-biting) excitement during the NHL playoffs."[10]

Summing up the success of multiple campaigns, Fairbank stated, "Brands and marketers are at an inflection point, and the winners will have both a great story to tell and highly targeted opportunities to engage consumers in more relevant ways, spend efficiently at scale, and measure and maximize their investments in real-time."

Building Careers of the Nation's Best Talent

Though not usually one to brag, Fairbank loses all self-control when talking about his employees. "Our highest calling has always been to attract and inspire the world's best talent. Our people are the heart of Capital One," Fairbank asserts. "Our associates bring diverse experiences and perspectives to the office, and they serve our customers and communities with generosity and ingenuity. They make Capital One special, and I am incredibly fortunate to lead such a talented team."

In 2018, Capital One added over 9,000 associates to this team. Of those, more than 1,000 were recent college graduates. Among these hires were thousands of engineers, data scientists, designers, product managers, and cyber professionals. Fairbank was quick to point out not all came from banking. Rather, he said, "Thousands of others brought experience and expertise in areas such as finance, operations, and customer care." In addition to hiring, Capital One focused on training, and has one of the most highly regarded technology internship programs in the nation. In addition, it also offers a Technology Development Program (TDP). TDP is a two-year rotational accelerator for high-performing software, data, and cybersecurity engineers.

In the beginning of 2018, Capital One added three new independent board members whose experiences and expertise were rooted in technology and innovation, rather than banking alone. Fairbank proudly introduced them in his annual letter:

Aparna Chennapragada is Vice President, Augmented Reality at Google, and she is a respected expert in artificial intelligence, machine learning, and mobile strategy. Eli Leenaars is Vice Chairman of the Global Wealth Management Division at UBS Group AG with thirty years of experience in financial services, including overseeing the remarkable growth of ING Direct in the US. He brings tremendous perspective about how our industry will be reinvented through the use of data, technology, and brand. François Locoh-Donou is the President and CEO of F5 Networks, Inc., and brings nearly two decades of experience in enterprise technology and building and managing a wide range of global products, teams, and operations. We are thrilled to welcome these leaders to Capital One, and their breadth of experiences will be invaluable as we continue our transformative technology and digital journey.

> **In addition to hiring, Capital One focused on training, and has one of the most highly regarded technology internship programs in the nation.**

Building a Diverse and Inclusive Workforce

Attracting great talent was only part of their mission. Fairbank had a long commitment to education and empowerment of his employees, and prefers to refer to them as *associates* of his. He is proud to state that he offers associates a base pay of $15 per hour for all US-based roles and has committed to increasing the representation of women and people of color across the organization to build a diverse and inclusive workplace. He has implemented seven thriving Business Resource Groups (BRGs), communities of associates, partners, and allies that support Capital One's growing diverse and underrepresented populations. Fairbank adds, "Our seven Business Resource Groups were created to support Capital One's growing diverse populations. These groups help attract, retain, and develop diverse talent: people who are driving our company forward."[11]

In 2018, Capital One received numerous awards and recognitions for its dedication to their employees. It received the honor of once again being added to *Fortune*'s "100 Best Companies to Work for," "World's Most Admired Companies," "100 Best Workplaces for Diversity," "100 Best Workplaces for Millennials," and "50 Best Workplaces for Parents" lists. It received the Human Rights Campaign Foundation "Corporate Equality Index of 100 Percent," the National Business Inclusion Consortium named Capital One "Best-of-the-Best Corporation for Inclusion," and Women's Choice named Capital One one of the "Best Companies for Multicultural Women." G.I. Jobs named Capital One a "Military-Friendly Employer (Silver)."

Fairbank, while proud, was not surprised by the accolades. "We've always gone to extraordinary lengths to recruit great people and give them a workplace where they can be great—as associates, leaders, family members, and citizens. We attract people who want to excel, grow, and be rewarded for their performance. We've created a culture where collaboration and openness matter and hierarchy doesn't, and where people are expected to do the right thing." An employee who didn't want to be named, but who is a veteran and has worked at the company for several years can attest to this. "Everyone is always doing the right thing. Asking: *Is this the right thing?* Even when speaking to each other there is no sense of hierarchy. Just respect. If you wouldn't talk to your mom, dad, aunt, friend in a certain way, you wouldn't talk that way at Capital One. In all my years, I've never heard a disrespectful word. And it comes from the leadership. It comes from the top." Reminiscing about the company, she recalled a moment that indicated just how deep the respect goes. She detailed a conversation between an associate and an HR officer (several years ago). The associate went to the HR director and said he needed his partner to be on his life insurance. Without fanfare, Capital One quickly instituted a policy that stated partners—regardless of gender or orientation or marriage—could be covered. Long before society mandated it, Capital One instituted it. "It was the right thing to do," the associate says. "So if it's the right thing, the conversation is simple."

> **❝** We've always gone to extraordinary lengths to recruit great people and give them a workplace where they can be great— as associates, leaders, family members, and citizens. We attract people who want to excel, grow, and be rewarded for their performance. We've created a culture where collaboration and openness matter and hierarchy doesn't, and where people are expected to do the right thing."

Fairbank, a father of eight who is active in his own kids' lives, understands the need for flexibility as well. "We understand that every person who comes to work has another life and sometimes needs a bit of flexibility or support—because of a family illness, for example, or to volunteer in the community," Fairbank adds. An employee who has sat in meetings with Fairbank has said he will excuse himself from work or a meeting for one of his children's events. Because of this, associates feel they too can be flexible. "He trusts us. We all trust each other to get the work done," an employee adds.

Building a Community

Capital One also has shown a commitment from the beginning to community programs and partnerships that helped to integrate Capital One's core strengths with the skills, expertise, and experiences. As a financial services company, they focused primarily on what Fairbank called "spurring economic growth and creating opportunities for many." In 2018, Capital One associates volunteered over 422,000 hours and donated some $44 million to nonprofits that help build economic opportunity in our communities. Through their FutureEdge community grants program, they invested $150 million over five years in job skills development; small business technology solutions; and personal financial tools and information. One of our FutureEdge partnerships was with Year Up, a nonprofit organization that provided young adults with the "skills, experience, and support to attain professional careers and higher education." Through Year Up, Capital One hired participants as interns, with former Year Up interns now working as fulltime associates. In partnership with local public schools and organizations, the Capital

One Coders program helped middle school students develop a greater interest in science, technology, engineering and mathematics (STEM). In the 10-week program, Capital One associate volunteers taught students in schools across the country about problem solving, teamwork, and the basic principles of software development and coding. Other workforce development programs supported by FutureEdge included Per Scholas (technology access and education for underserved communities), Future Founders (entrepreneurship skills for high school students), and Dress for Success (economic independence for women). In 2018, Capital One received awards for their efforts in the community including *Fortune*'s "Best 50 Workplaces for Giving Back."

> In 2018, Capital One associates volunteered over 422,000 hours and donated some $44 million to nonprofits that help build economic opportunity in our communities.

Building a Sustainable and Eco-Friendly Business

From the beginning, one of Capital One's core principles and values was rooted in what they called their "sense of accountability" for their actions, both to their stakeholders and society as a whole. Fairbank stated, "We are committed to continuously improving the environmental sustainability of our business, to reducing the impact of our operations, and to using resources and materials thoughtfully. We continue to engage our associates, customers, suppliers, and other stakeholders in our environmental efforts." Some of their efforts included purchasing 100 percent renewable energy (purchasing 317,000 MWh of Renewable Energy Credits (RECs) in 2018) and aiming for carbon neutral building. They also aimed to cut business travel greenhouse gas emissions as well. Capital One committed to reducing landfill waste 50 percent by 2025 at their four primary campus locations. At those locations, they have removed all individual trash cans and implemented centralized waste bins that include composting and recycling. In 2018, they composted 1,137 tons of organic waste, recycled 714 tons of secure shred paper, and recycled 740 tons of plastics, nonconfidential paper, and aluminum. They also donate food that otherwise might go to waste to local hunger relief organizations (more than 16 tons of food was donated in 2018).[12]

Between 2015 and 2018, Capital One invested more than $7 billion in environmentally responsible projects through their renewable energy, multi-family green financing, and not-for-profit banking businesses. Additionally, they installed an on-site solar array at their 1717 Innovation Center in Richmond, Virginia. Fairbank added, "We believe that renewable energy is a critical tool in the fight against climate change and in 2018 Capital One joined other leading global companies and became a member of RE100, a global initiative of businesses committed to 100 percent renewable electricity. We recently set new goals for reducing greenhouse gas emissions."[13]

Speaking of long-term sustainability goals, Fairbank stated, "We are carbon neutral for Scope 1, Scope 2 and business travel emissions, and we committed to a 25 percent reduction in Scope 3 emissions by 2025 from a 2018 baseline. Scope 1 GHG emissions are direct emissions from sources that are owned or controlled by Capital One; Scope 2 GHG emissions are indirect emissions from energy purchased by Capital One; and Scope 3 emissions are from sources that are not owned or directly controlled by Capital One but are related to our activities such as our supply chain, associate commute and business travel. We inventory and verify our GHG emissions each year through a reputable third party and report them annually to CDP."[14]

Capital One also pursued US Green Building Council's Leadership in Energy and Environmental Design (LEED) Silver (or higher) certification for all new office construction and comprehensive renovations. More than 50 percent of their office portfolio is currently LEED or Green Globe certified, including the new McLean 2 building, located in Tysons, Virginia, which has a variety of eco-friendly features including: rainwater capture, green roof vegetation, electric-vehicle charging ports, native plant landscaping, automated shade and lighting controls for daylight harvesting, and access to public transportation and bike racks.[15]

By 2019, Capital One had secured itself solidly as a vision-oriented tech company that happened to be a bank, but it was much more than that. It became a key player and stakeholder in their local communities, the lives of its associates, and an integral part of the customers well-being. They also showed a commitment in every area—talent, technology, brand building, community service, sustainability, diversity, workplace satisfaction, and product excellence—to "do the right thing."

New Ventures

Twenty-five years ago, Richard Fairbank and Nigel Morris started a company and their mission then is every bit what it is today: "Let's do something great together." Their goal all along was a simple one—cut the price of credit and allow more people to have access to it—but it was also cloaked by a willingness to disrupt the old way of doing things and make way for a new way to conduct business as usual. They wanted, as their website proclaims, to "bring ingenuity, simplicity, and humanity to an industry ripe for change."

In those twenty-five years as a public company, Capital One has come a *very* long way. They started as a small, credit card startup into one of the largest, fastest-growing, most visible, and most innovative companies in America. According to Fairbank, however, the Capital One story was built upon millions of little stories, "An immigrant building her credit and buying a home. A twenty-two-year-old software engineer accepting a job to join a bank (of all things!) after graduation. And a small business owner using his Spark rewards card to pay for his employees' healthcare." These stories are the hallmark of the company and why Morris and Fairbank got started in the first place. They were two men who wanted to not only disrupt an industry, and use data to do so, but they wanted to, above all, "do the right thing."

What started as a seed of an idea became a full-fledged company that helped transform peoples' lives. Since 1994, the world has been through enormous social, economic, political, and cultural changes. Together we all watched the Towers collapse on 9/11, we watched our family members go off to war, we watched as our economy struggled, wobbled, flourished, and struggled yet again. We lived through the tech bubble, the real estate bubble, the Great Recession, and political and social upheaval.

Beyond all that, we all had a front row seat to witness the dawn of the digital age. In 1994, when the first bulky mobile phones were showing up in movies and occasionally in the hands of a "very important person" on the streets of Manhattan, it was hard to imagine then that we would be accessing our bank accounts, making online stock trades, and even paying for our coffees with our phones. Few people had the vision. And even fewer still had the courage to take that vision and make it into a reality. Richard Fairbank and Nigel Morris had that vision, and Richard Fairbank, like his own father, is still committed to seeing far into a future, a future few can imagine. He's confident in that future: "We've seen enormous change in our culture and our society, but the change that took place over Capital One's first twenty-five years will pale in comparison to the quarter century that's about to unfold. And we are well-positioned to thrive as technology changes everything. I am inspired by our customers who trust us to serve them each day with both wisdom and humanity. And I am humbled by the opportunity to lead 50,000 associates who are all-in to change banking for good."

O ver the years, Fairbank developed and honed the now proprietary information based strategy—IBS—which became
the mainstay of Capital One's company strategy throughout the
past twenty-five years. Using advanced information technology
and sophisticated quantitative analysis, Capital One gathered vast
amounts of data about their current and potential customers all
in the hopes to better serve them. By designing and pricing products to fit each customer's financial circumstances, Capital One
was able to add almost seven million customers within the first
few years of their company's start and is now one of the Top 10
banks in the United States. Relying on data and looking at their
company not so much as a "bank" but an "tech company" proved
to be a successful approach. They also looked ahead. Using what
Fairbank called his "Gretzky Concept," he was always looking
far out into the future and never settling for the status quo.

Relying on data, not limiting themselves to thinking they
were just a "credit card" company or a "bank," and looking far
out into the future were key drivers to their ultimate success.

Below are seven lessons that you can take away from Capital
One:

1. *Have a mindset dedicated to constant innovation and refuse
   to accept the status quo.* One of the key not-so-secret se-

crets to Capital One's success is an innovation mindset. As Fairbank said, "We believe that every business or product idea has a limited shelf life." Every product they built, they built with the end in mind. Fairbank managed to stay ahead of downtrends by constantly being on the lookout for new and up-and-coming opportunities. Capital One was the first bank in the nation to offer balance transfer products nationwide. However, it eventually drew competitors and, over time his approach became less profitable. Fairbank was counting on that, and planned for it with a suite of what he called "second generation" products, such as secured cards, college student cards, affinity cards, and a variety of cards for underserved markets. Planning for the future, looking far out ahead, and being on the vanguard of new and upcoming trends is vital to staying profitable. Companies have to be willing to change, create new products, and even let go of ones no longer working.

2. *Use an information based strategy and data to make decisions, not gut feelings or whims, or anecdotal evidence in order to mitigate risk.* Fairbank credited the information based strategy in giving them the ability to make "opportunistic moves even with mature products" and to mitigate risk. Fairbank used data and the tools to manage risk effectively. Capital One uses sophisticated models to analyze risk, and base their decisions on what Fairbank calls "highly conservative" forecasts. The combination of this strategy and their overall conservatism has been critical to their performance, even during economic downturns. While the hallmark of Capital One's strategy has been aggressive growth

through innovation, it secured their position in the marketplace through its culture of conservatism. While these two concepts—innovation and conservatism—may seem antithetical, to Fairbank they are not. Though highly invested in innovation, Capital One relies on the rigorous discipline of testing. Only new products that have demonstrated an ability to superior returns are launched. They measure and predict what Fairbank calls "inevitable" declines of existing opportunities and constantly challenge the organization to find new sources of growth. In addition, they are conservative with their own balance sheets and are careful to keep large financial buffers to help them weather adverse conditions outside of their control.

3. *Invest in technology.* Also important to Capital One's strong growth was their use of cutting-edge information technology and using it to create a highly flexible operating infrastructure. From the beginning Fairbank knew how integral technology was to his business strategy. He built a solid infrastructure in-house that allowed them to bring new ideas to market much more quickly than their competition. As the information revolution increasingly transformed other consumer products and services, Fairbank never wavered in his belief that strategy and technology would enable them to seize a competitive advantage in the marketplace. It wasn't just the technology itself that Capital One invested in, but a technology focused culture. In addition to agile management, Capital One adopted a DevOps culture with the "You Built It, You Own It" mindset. It's designed to quickly deliver features, fixes, and updates, and requires that teams work collaboratively

from beginning to end. Though they are by every means a large corporation, they are still operating every bit like a small software startup.

4. *Establish core values and principles from the outset.* Capital One's sustained success, Fairbank contends, is the product of a set of principles they have embraced since bringing the information-based strategy IBS to Signet in 1988. These principles, the essence of Capital One, combined strategic insights and management values, were not just something they talked about; they were and are a way of life at Capital One. The principles are woven into the fabric of the company, and have been a part of it since day one. Besides relying on data to help make key decisions, they also believe in "doing the right thing" in every manner of business. And "doing the right thing" at its core starts with the leadership. What goes for those at the top, is the same for everyone in the company. Another essential principle and value at the core of Capital One is communication. They believe in honest, forthright, direct, yet, gracious communication from "top-down, bottom-up, and across departments."

5. *Recruit the best of the best.* Besides IBS and utilizing technology, one of their core principles was recruiting. The complexity of their strategy and unending innovation demanded what Fairbank calls "world-class talent" and "intellectual and executional superstars." Just as they used IBS to enhance credit offerings, they used them to find the best candidates and measure their performance through comprehensive tests and interviews. Anyone who works at Capital One or who has been through the rigorous process, which includes not just

one but several interviews, knows that the standards are extraordinarily high. Senior management is extensively involved throughout the recruiting process. After hiring the best of the best, they work hard to develop them through training programs, exposure to management, coaching, job rotation, and early opportunities for unusually broad responsibility. Career development efforts are seen as critical in building the competencies required by Capital One's information-based strategy. The information-based strategy begins with hiring exceptional talent—who are eager to seize challenges, to take ownership as soon as problems arise, and to make solutions happen.

6. *Create a culture that supports growth and success.* Capital One believes that employees need the proper environment to support "peak performance" and they have created a culture of entrepreneurship, which is distinctive in a large corporation. Capital One encourages its associates to "think and act like owners." They challenge their managers to see themselves not as bosses but as coaches dedicated "to empowering every player by providing direction, leading by example, setting extraordinary standards, and keeping our very fast track clear of the usual bureaucratic barriers to high performance." Capital One has spread the spirit of ownership throughout the company by making all associates eligible for their employee stock ownership program, as well as their 401(K) plan, and stock options.

7. *Invest in Branding.* Capital One has, from the beginning, invested in their brand. From their earliest years, they worked tirelessly to set themselves apart from other banks and credit cards in the industry. In 2018

they spent $2.2 billion on marketing and advertising, virtually unmatched in the industry. Over the years they have hired iconic and well-known celebrities— Alec Baldwin, Jennifer Garner, and Samuel L. Jackson to tout the merits of their cards. They sponsor sporting events: NCAA Final Four, the Florida Citrus Bowl, and the Capital One Arena, home of the Capitals. They have also made several strategic acquisitions across the county to grow their brand and name recognition. Though their name is practically synonymous with credit cards now, they haven't scaled back their branding and marketing efforts and continue to invest heavily in it.

ENDNOTES

Introduction

1. Robert Wright, *One Nation Under Debt: Hamilton, Jefferson, and the History of What We Owe,* (New York: McGraw-Hill, 2008).
2. Alex Silady, "The Top Ten Banks in America," Smart Asset, November 20, 2018, https://smartasset.com/checking-account/the-top-ten-banks-by-assets-held.
3. Victor Zarnowitz, *Business Cycles: Theory, History, Indicators, and Forecasting,* (Chicago: University of Chicago, 1996), 211-226.
4. Peter High, "How Capital One Became a Leading Digital Bank," Forbes.com, December 12, 2016, https://www.forbes.com/sites/peterhigh/2016/12/12/how-capital-one-became-a-leading-digital-bank/#12062a1215ee.
5. Peter High.
6. Stanford University Graduate School of Business, Case Study: SM-135, "Capital One: Setting and Shaping Strategy," December 17, 2004.
7. Fortune.com, https://fortune.com/best-companies/2019/search/?company=Capital%20One.

Chapter 1

1. Stanford University Graduate School of Business, Case Study: SM-135, "Capital One: Setting and Shaping Strategy," December 17, 2004.
2. All subsequent quotes from Nigel Morris come from a recorded interview at Startup Grind Washington, DC, YouTube, https://www.youtube.com/watch?v=InEjXJWrqvk.

3. Elizabeth Dexheimer, "What's in Capital One's CEO's Wallet? An $800 Million Dollar Fortune," Bloomberg.com, June 24, 2015, https://www.bloomberg.com/news/articles/2015-06-24/what-s-in-fairbank-s-wallet-a-fortune-from-building-capital-one.

4. Jane Davenport Fairbank, Obituary, legacy.com, July 1, 2003, https://www.legacy.com/obituaries/mercurynews/obituary.aspx?n=jane-davenport-fairbank&pid=1177406.

5. Walter Sullivan, "Prof. William N. Fairbank, Physicist and Pioneer in Quarks," *New York Times*, October 3, 1989, https://www.nytimes.com/1989/10/03/obituaries/prof-william-n-fairbank-72-physicist-and-pioneer-in-quarks.html?pagewanted=1.

6. Dexheimer.

7. Dexheimer.

8. Capital One Annual Report, 1996, https://ir-capitalone.gcs-web.com/static-files/d823fcd3-e1f1-439a-a34f-5296ef58b93c.

9. Stanford University Case Study, December 17, 2004.

10. Stanford, 2004.

11. Stanford, 2004.

12. Stanford, 2004.

13. Stanford, 2004.

14. Stanford, 2004.

15. Stanford, 2004.

16. Stanford, 2004.

17. Nanette Byrnes, "Coming of Age at Capital One: After a Regulatory Scare Management Realizes that the Startup Era is Over," Bloomberg Business, February 16, 2004, https://www.bloomberg.com/news/articles/2004-02-15/coming-of-age-at-capital-one.

18. Nanette Byrnes.

19. Loren, Fox, "Capital Two," Institutional Investor, January 10, 2007, https://www.institutionalinvestor.com/article/b150nxks0gc0k3/capital-two.

20. Stanford University Case Study, December 17, 2004.

21. Harvard Business School Case Study, "Capital One Financial Corporation," April 24, 2000, pp. 5–6.

22. Harvard, 5-6.

23. Harvard, 5-6.

24. Dave Murphy, "Richard Fairbank: 'Nobody Wants to Work for a Phony,'" Stanford.edu, November 1, 2007, https://www.gsb

.stanford.edu/insights/richard-fairbank-nobody-wants-work -phony.

25. Stanford University Case Study, December 17, 2004.
26. Connie Prater, "Who Gets Credit Cards May Be a Matter of Black and White," creditcards.com, June 4, 2008, https://www .creditcards.com/credit-card-news/credit-card-discrimination -1276.php.
27. Stanford University Case Study, December 17, 2004.
28. Murphy.
29. Murphy.
30. Capital One Annual Report, 1996, https://ir-capitalone.gcs-web .com/static-files/d823fcd3-e1f1-439a-a34f-5296ef58b93c.
31. Capital One, 1996.
32. Capital One, 1996.
33. Capital One, 1996.
34. Capital One, 1996.
35. Capital One, 1996.
36. Capital One, 1996.
37. Capital One, 1996.
38. Capital One, 1996.
39. Capital One, 1996.
40. Capital One, 1996.
41. Stanford University Case Study, December 17, 2004.
42. John Levensque, "The Creatives: Keith Goldberg," Seattle Business, August 2015, https://www.seattlebusinessmag.com/article /creatives-keith-goldberg.
43. "Madison Avenue Advertising Walk of Fame Announces 2011 Inductees," Business Wire, October 4, 2011, https://www.business wire.com/news/home/20111004006326/en/Madison-Avenue -Advertising-Walk-Fame-Announces-2011.
44. Nigel Morris Biography, QED Investors, https://qedinvestors .com/team/nigel-morris/.
45. Murphy.

Chapter 2

1. Capital One: Visigoths. Commercial, published December 21, 2000, https://adage.com/creativity/work/visigoths/13068?.

2. Eric Dash, "Chief of Capital One Applies Hockey Strategies to Banking," *New York Times,* July 10, 2007, https://www.nytimes.com /2007/07/10/business/10bank.html.

3. Dash.

4. Loren, Fox, "Capital Two," Institutional Investor, January 10, 2007, https://www.institutionalinvestor.com/article/b150nxks 0gc0k3/capital-two.

5. "New Market Force Banking Study: Capital One is Consumer's Favorite, Satisfaction and Loyalty is Down Industry Wide," Lou-isville, Colorado, Oct. 25, 2017, https://www.marketforce.com /2017-market-force-banking-customer-survey.

6. "Capital One Plans Purchase of Auto Financing Company," Bloomberg News, July 17, 1998, https://www.nytimes.com/1998 /07/17/business/company-news-capital-one-plans-purchase -of-auto-financing-company.html.

7. Fox.

8. Fox.

9. "Capital One Financial Agrees to Acquire PeopleFirst, Inc.; Ex-pands Auto Financing Business," press release, September 21, 2001, http://phx.corporate-ir.net/phoenix.zhtml?c=251626&p =irol-newsArticle&ID=1858167.

10. Capital One Press Release, September 21, 2001.

11. "PeopleFirst Changes Brand to Capital One Auto Finance," The Auto Channel, press release, June 27, 2003, https://www.theauto channel.com/news/2003/06/27/163894.html.

12. Auto Channel Press Release, June 27, 2003.

13. "Groundbreaking Credit Card Rates Are No Longer Just Short Term," press release, July 9, 2003, https://ir-capitalone.gcs-web .com/news-releases/news-release-details/groundbreaking -credit-card-rates-are-no-longer-just-short-term?ID=429567 &c=70667&p=irol-newsArticle_Print.

14. "Capital One Reports Second Quarter Earnings per Share In-crease of 34% Over Year Ago Period," press release, July 16, 2003, http://phx.corporate-ir.net/phoenix.zhtml?c=251626&p =irol-newsArticle&ID=1858231.

15. "Capital One Partners with Leading Author Robert Hammond to Educate Americans on Combating the Fastest Growing Crime in America," press release, September 24, 2003, http://phx

.corporate-ir.net/phoenix.zhtml?c=251626&p=irol-news
Article&ID=1858254.

16. "New Survey Shows Teenagers Want Financial Advice from Parents," press release, October 23, 2003, http://phx.corporate
-ir.net/phoenix.zhtml?c=251626&p=irol-newsArticle&ID
=1858258.

17. "Capital One and Consumer Action Sponsor Free Financial
Seminar for 80 Local Non-Profit Community Organizations,"
press release, November 18, 2003, http://phx.corporate-ir.net
/phoenix.zhtml?c=251626&p=irol-newsArticle&ID=1858263.

18. "Help for Consumers Considering Bankruptcy," press release,
November 24, 2003, http://phx.corporate-ir.net/phoenix.zhtml
?c=251626&p=irol-newsArticle&ID=1858264.

19. "Capital One and Consumer Action Launch MoneyWi$e Website," press release, March 8, 2004, http://phx.corporate-ir.net
/phoenix.zhtml?c=251626&p=irol-newsArticle&ID=1858274.

20. "Capital One's New Go Miles Offers Travelers Unmatched Flexibility and No Hassle Rewards," press release, January 13, 2004,
http://phx.corporate-ir.net/phoenix.zhtml?c=251626&p=irol
-newsArticle&ID=1858268.

21. "Regulators Terminate Memorandum of Understanding," press
release, January 29, 2004, http://phx.corporate-ir.net/phoenix
.zhtml?c=251626&p=irol-newsArticle&ID=1858270.

22. Nanette Byrnes, "Coming of Age at Capital One: After a Regulatory Scare Management Realizes that the Startup Era is Over,"
Bloomberg Business, February 16, 2004, https://www.bloomberg
.com/news/articles/2004-02-15/coming-of-age-at-capital-one.

23. Nanette Byrnes.

24. Nanette Byrnes.

Chapter 3

1. Loren Fox, "Capital Two," *Institutional Investor,* January 10, 2007,
https://www.institutionalinvestor.com/article/b150nxks0gc
0k3/capital-two.

2. Fox.

3. Fox.

4. Fox.

5. Fox.

6. Fox.

7. Fox.

8. Fox.

9. Fox.

10. "Capital One Closes Wholesale Mortgage Unit," press release, August 20, 2007, http://phx.corporate-ir.net/phoenix.zhtml?c =251626&p=irol-newsArticle&ID=1858483.

11. Fox.

12. "Capital One Reports Third Quarter Earnings per Share (dilute) of $1.00," press release, October 16, 2008, http://phx.corporate -ir.net/phoenix.zhtml?c=251626&p=irol-newsArticle&ID =1858546.

13. Capital One, 2008.

14. Capital One Annual Report, 2009, https://ir-capitalone.gcs-web .com/static-files/007611b5-8927-45bf-8dec-a0da78075519.

15. Capital One, 2009.

16. Capital One, 2009.

17. Capital One, 2009.

18. Capital One, 2009.

19. Capital One, 2009.

20. Capital One, 2009.

21. Capital One, 2009.

22. Capital One, 2009.

23. Capital One, 2009.

24. Capital One, 2009.

25. Capital One, 2009.

26. Capital One, 2009.

27. Capital One, 2009.

28. Capital One, 2009.

29. Capital One, 2009.

30. Capital One, 2009.

31. Capital One, 2009.

32. Ben Protess and Michael De La Merced, "Frank Questions Capital One's Deal for ING Online Bank," Dealbook, *New York Times*, August 18, 2011, https://dealbook.nytimes.com/2011/08/18 /frank-questions-capital-ones-deal-for-ing-online-bank/.

33. Ben Protess, Michael De La Merced.

34. Ben Protess, Michael De La Merced.

35. Ben Protess, Michael De La Merced.

36. "Capital One Completes Acquisition of ING Direct," press release, February 17, 2012, http://phx.corporate-ir.net/phoenix .zhtml?c=251626&p=irol-newsArticle&ID=1858727.

37. Capital One Press Release, February 17, 2012.

38. "Capital One Recognized by J.D. Power and Associates for Outstanding Customer Service," press release, February 7, 2012, http://phx.corporate-ir.net/phoenix.zhtml?c=251626&p=irol -newsArticle&ID=1858726.

39. "Capital One Recognized as One of America's Top 50 Community-Minded Companies," press release, November 8, 2012, http://phx.corporate-ir.net/phoenix.zhtml?c=251626&p =irol-newsArticle&ID=1858768.

Chapter 4

1. All interviews for subsequent quotes with Chris Zadeh were conducted by the author in Amsterdam in 2019.

2. Capital One Annual Report, 2012, https://ir-capitalone.gcs-web .com/static-files/a1ed7374-bc9a-4c9e-ae89-d67af3400147.

3. Capital One, 2012.

4. Capital One, 2012.

5. Capital One, 2012.

6. Capital One, 2012.

7. Capital One, 2012.

8. Capital One, 2012.

9. Capital One, 2012.

10. Capital One, 2012.

11. Capital One, 2012.

12. Capital One, 2012.

13. "NCRP Statement Casts Doubt Over Capital One's Commitment to Philanthropy: Philanthropy Watchdog to Testify Before the Federal Reserve over the Capital One-ING Direct Merger," press release, Washington, DC, October 4, 2011, https://web.archive .org/web/20140306214057/http://www.ncrp.org/news-room /press-releases/776-doubt-over-capital-ones-commitment-to -philanthropy-.

14. Capital One Annual Report, 2012.

15. Capital One, 2012.

Chapter 5

1. Daniel Senovitz, "What's in Capital One's New Tyson's Headquarters? Pretty Much Everything," *Washington Business Journal*, November 2, 2018, https://www.bizjournals.com/washington/news/2018/11/02/whats-in-capital-ones-new-tysons-headquarters.html.

2. Capital One Annual Report, 2018, https://ir-capitalone.gcs-web.com/static-files/04c57bd9-b351-418c-9f18-ed91d4bfad23.

3. Capital One, 2018.

4. Rob McLean, "A Hacker Gained Access to 100 Million Capital One Credit Card Applications and Accounts," CNN Business, July 30, 2019, https://www.cnn.com/2019/07/29/business/capital-one-data-breach/index.html.

5. "What We Know About Accused Capital One Breach Hacker," July 30, 2019, https://www.cbsnews.com/news/paige-thompson-what-we-know-about-accused-capital-one-breach-hacker-2019-07-31/.

6. April Glaser, "Capital One Took Nearly Two Weeks to Disclose Its Hack and Customers Still Don't Know if They Were Affected," Slate, July 31, 2019, https://slate.com/technology/2019/07/capital-one-hack-no-customer-notification.html.

7. "Capital One Announces Data Security Incident," July 29, 2019, https://www.capitalone.com/about/newsroom/capital-one-announces-data-security-incident/.

8. Capital One Annual Report, 2018.

9. Capital One, 2018.

10. Capital One, 2018.

11. Capital One, 2018.

12. Capital One, 2018.

13. Capital One, 2018.

14. Capital One, 2018.

15. Capital One, 2018.

INDEX

Read on for the
Introduction from

THE
SEPHORA
STORY

Available now from HarperCollins Leadership

INTRODUCTION

Very few industries and retailers these days can say they are "Amazon-proof" or even "Recession-proof." That is unless you're in the global cosmetics business, which is expected to grow 7 percent a year over the next three years—reaching 806 billion dollars by 2023, according to Orbis Research.[1] Companies like Sephora, and its competitors, Ulta, Dermstore, Nordstrom, and Macy's, are no exception. In fact, since its founding in 1969 by Dominique Mandonnaud, Sephora has grown from a small perfume shop in Paris to one of the leading beauty product retailers in the world. Beauty product retailers like them, which carry cosmetics, skin care, body care, fragrance, nail color, beauty supplements, styling and beauty tools seem to be impervious to the ebbs and flows of the economy. When other industries and companies have floundered to stay afloat, Sephora has adapted, innovated, and risen above.

Some argue the reason the beauty industry, as a whole, is thriving is because of all the rampant societal pressure and norms that increasingly suggest that *younger is better*. Globally we are seeing an increased aging population[2] who simply can't abide wrinkles, dry skin, blotchy skin tones, freckles, age spots, adult acne, thinning brows, upper lip fuzz, broken, damaged, or graying hair, or any other unseemly looks on the "beauty don't lists." It's not just the aging populations that are feeling the heat and raising the demand for more advanced beauty products. With the widespread use of social media—YouTube, Facebook, Instagram, Twitter, Snapchat, and TikTok—it's nearly impossible for young people to escape the social pressure to appear beautiful at all times. Some critics even go so far as to blame the cosmetic and beauty industries for raising the standards of beauty in order to market and prey on an unsuspecting public. While the beauty industry isn't completely blameless, it's not solely responsible either. The desire to be young and beautiful dates further back than the inception of Instagram, or even the makeup counter, for that fact. Companies like Sephora have found success not because they have marketed or preyed upon the insecurities of individuals, but rather they have anticipated their deepest needs, desires, and hopes and responded in kind. Well aware that feeling beautiful is more than skin deep and is an intrinsic desire, Sephora meets its customers where there are.

In fact, the name *Sephora* harkens back to beauty's historical (or more accurately literary and etymological) origins. Sephora is a mashup of *sephos*, which means beauty in Greek, and *Zipporah*, which was the name of the Biblical Moses's beautiful wife, whose name in Greek is spelled *Sepphora*.

The desire to be look and *feel* beautiful and youthful is not something Madison Avenue advertising agencies and cosmetic companies invented. Long before Insta influencers were trying on mascara and making serum recs, in prehistoric times red ochre was used as a way to decorate the skin (and discovered in excavated graves of our female genetic ancestors) and over a thousand years ago women and men painted their eyes with kohl, sprayed perfume, used red rouge lipstick,[3] and soaked in warm baths of milk and honey. The desire to luxuriate, accentuate one's most beautiful features, satisfy the senses, or even change one's look has been a driving force in humanity for eons.

A Very Brief History of Makeup: "I Am Ready for My Close-up, Mr. DeMille"

Though the desire to be beautiful may be as old as civilization itself, Teresa Riordan's 2004 book, *Inventing Beauty,* argues that as photography became more popular and widespread (somewhere after 1870) cosmetics did as well. Prior to this, makeup was reserved for the tawdrier members of society, i.e. the euphemistically called "Ladies of the night," and of course, thespians whose faces needed to stand out under the harsh lighting and seen from the back of theatre. But with the rise of photography and cinema, cosmetics became mainstream. As early as the 1880s, many budding entrepreneurs saw the opportunity to create cosmetics so their customers could look as beautiful as the women in the magazines and advertising. Most of these companies were independently owned and operated by women—the most popular being the California Perfume Company, which later became Avon. Individual agents—mostly women—sold beautifying creams, lotions, and facial tints to their friends and family members. This unique business model allowed women to become more financially independent. It also meant that with more women working in the cosmetics industry there was more money to spend on cosmetics. It's a win-win formula that still is winning today for similar tier-marketing cosmetic companies like Mary Kay, Arbonne, and Beautycounter, which afford women the opportunity to earn money as entrepreneurs, cosmetic agents, and makeup artists.[4]

Even during serious economic downturns, cosmetic sales steadily increased.[5] Where other industries completely collapsed, makeup was a simple, small luxury a woman could afford in desperate times. Instead of rationalizing buying a dress or a pair of shoes to feel pretty, a woman could simply purchase an inexpensive tube of lipstick and feel instantly glamorous.

Modern Cosmetics and the Beauty Industry

By the early 1900s, however, makeup had become a mainstay, not to mention part of the lexicon. Perhaps the most notable makeup artist of this era and the founding father of the modern cosmetics industry is Max Factor. In the early 1900s, he was a famed wigmaker and face artist for Hollywood studios and he developed a "greasepaint" foundation that didn't crack or flake off.[6] It was an instant sensation. It wasn't long before actresses began wearing it offscreen as well. Factor went on to develop lip gloss and eyebrow pencils, and "pan-cake" compact of powdered foundation called "Pan-Cake Brand Make Up." Many attribute the term *makeup* (now just one word) to him because of this. It's considered the first time the term is seen or used in media advertising. By the 1920s, he took his products to the mass market with a promise to his female customers that they too could look like movie stars. Ad copy along with featured stars like Judy Garland, Rita Hayworth, Lana Turner, Merle Oberon, and Ella Raines, promised "This is make-up that actually creates glamour . . . . The Screen Star Secret that beautifies instantly." Who wouldn't want to look like Rita Hayworth or Lana Turner?

Max Factor hit pay dirt. But, he wasn't the only one.

Around the same time in 1915, T.L. Williams started Maybelline Company, though at first it was only an eye-makeup company. In truth, the makeup was his sister Mabel's idea, or rather a result of her resourcefulness. After singeing her lashes off by accident, she mixed coal dust and Vaseline and applied to what was left of her lashes to duplicate the look of real ones. She discovered she could make them look even longer, replicating the look of the big-eyed Hollywood starlets like Mary Pickford. A savvy businessman, her brother packaged the concoctions (without actual coal) in a tin and called it Lash-Brow-Ine. He named the brand itself Maybelline by combining *Mabel* and *Vaseline*.[7] Our idea of what constitutes an acceptable lash length has never been the same since. Thanks, Mabel.

For the first part of the twentieth century the makeup industry grew as the proliferation of women's magazines (which required ads for makeup and other popular items for women) also flourished. However, the *way* in which customers purchased and experienced makeup began to change by the end of World War II. Prior to this time period most makeup was typically available by mail order, behind the counter at department stores, or through independent agents. But thanks in large part to Estée Lauder, founder of the eponymous brand of makeup that still exists today, the cosmetic buying experience fundamentally changed. In 1946, Lauder began what was to become a massive makeup empire though a particularly revolutionary approach—by meeting women where they were. Or should we say, where they would be a captive audience to hearing about skincare. *Where was that?* At beauty salons of course. With women stuck under hair dryers, she gave away free samples as well as bonus gifts of the skin cream that she developed with her uncle. In addition to her unique marketing and sales approach, she allowed customers to interact with her products. Eventually Saks Fifth

Avenue placed an order, and it was there that she continued to give away free samples, added gifts, and focused on recurring personalized marketing techniques to build brand loyalty.[8] Her approach proved successful. Since launching the Estée Lauder brand in 1946, the Lauder family has expanded to include a number of popular brands as well, including but not limited to Bobbi Brown, Clinique, Origins, Glamglow, Prescriptives, La Mer, MAC, Smashbox, Too Faced, Aerin, Becca, haircare lines Aveda and Bumble and Bumble, and numerous fragrance lines. In many ways Lauder was the pioneer of the modern cosmetics industry, and paved the ways for stores like Sephora, which not only carry most of her brands today but also meets the customer where they are (not in beauty salons, but rather online, in store, on social media), offer free samples and free gifts with purchase, showcase interactive displays, as well as provide recurring personalized marketing and brand loyalty programs.

The modern cosmetics and beauty industry (and thankfully the science behind it) has come a long way, and not just from the days of Cleopatra's Egypt, but from Max Factor's "greasepaint" and "pan-cake" makeup tins as well. Gone are the days of painting one's face with poisonous ceruse and other hazardous lead- and arsenic-based methods. In addition to scientific and technological advances in the past 150 years, the entire beauty industry has grown exponentially and become an integral part of the growing global economy.

Sephora's Origin Story Linked to the Past

Sephora has been one of those companies leading the way for the past fifty years. They've been doing so both differently and better than their competitors thanks in part to their strategy, which Dominique Mandonnaud introduced when he opened his small perfume shop in Limoges, France, in 1969. Perhaps inspired by Estée Lauder's approach, or perhaps his own need and desire to interact with the product, Mandonnaud wanted to create an experiential encounter. Where he lived, most women and men shopping for perfumes were separated from the products by a counter, which was managed by a sales associate. There was very little experiential nature to the purchase. He wanted to interact with products when he shopped, and thought customers would want to too. He didn't just want to sell a product—he wanted to provide an experience. *Come in, walk up to the perfume, hold it in your hands, spray it on your own wrists, and savor it—maybe go home with a sample to try out for a day or two.* Though in 1969 there was no data to show, as there is today, just how compelling and effective this experience actually was in order to close a sale, Mandonnaud knew intuitively that this was where the beauty industry needed to go.

Much like Lauder, Mandonnaud believed the future of beauty meant removing the barriers between the customer and the product—and it meant meeting the customer where they were. Like Max Factor, Mandonnaud believed his customers should feel extremely special, as if they were walking onto a theatrical stage and playing the starring role in their own lives. In fact, up until 2018, the sales floor in Sephora was called *the stage,* and all the employees were referred to as *stage directors,* their black and red (now just black and white) uniforms were called *costumes,* the back area of the store was called *backstage,* and the customers were referred to as, you guessed it, *cast members.* Like Mabel Williams, Mandonnaud was resourceful and innovative, always looking for the newest and best ways to please and delight his customers. Though a lot has changed in the past few years for the cosmetic industry, especially with the rise of the digital age, Sephora hasn't loosened its foothold on the experiential component its stores offer.

What to Expect in This Book

In this book you will find out how Mandonnaud transformed a small perfume boutique into an international beauty retailer. You will learn how he and then his business partners and subsequent CEOs overcame obstacles all along the way. You'll also learn the strategies and practices they employed through the years to adapt to the fast-paced and competitive beauty industry. You'll learn how Sephora was on the vanguard of the beauty industry's role in the digital marketplace, and how they used innovative test-and-learn practices, high-tech tools, as well as data to transform the cosmetic and skincare buying experience. Finally, you'll find out how they dealt with pitfalls and major challenges, like lawsuits, scandals, diversity and inclusion issues, and how they plan to meet the ever-changing and evolving retail landscape in the future.

Ultimately, you will learn how Sephora has evolved and adapted to the digital age with a proven business model that is the envy not just of the cosmetics world, but of all retail. Sephora's unique strategy relies on data and technology to fully understand their customers' needs. Over the years, Sephora's commitment to cast members'—ahem, *customers'*—satisfaction has driven them to pioneer and create tech-enabled retail experiences. Like many innovative companies that rely on data and innovation—through test and learn iterations—Sephora is no exception. They continuously exceed the expectations of their customers and have held their own against massive competition—big box retailers, apparel retailers, department stores, niche clean beauty retailers, direct marketing retailers, online retailers, and even the great retail annihilator, Amazon.

Sephora is now the world's leading specialist perfume retailer, with over 2,600 stores in thirty-four countries.[9] They are also a beauty/cosmetic brand in their own right and have developed their own private, affordably priced label, Sephora Collection brand cosmetics, as well as the world-renowned anti-wrinkle and skincare product, StriVectin-SD. In addition to being a retailer, cosmetic brand, and skincare line, they have also expanded their services to offer in-store services, classes, and events, as well as provide fully interactive online communities as well. Now the subsidiary of luxury goods group LVMH Moët Hennessy Louis Vuitton S.A., which owns many of the brands positioned on Sephora's shelves, Sephora is the largest unit of LVMH's Selective Retailing Division, and has exceeded revenues of six billion dollars and has no plans to slow down anytime soon.

The future is within reach.

When you start making your goals a top priority, everything falls into place. Learn from the leaders inspiring millions & apply their strategies to your professional journey.

Leadership Essentials Blog

Activate 180 Podcast

Interactive E-courses

Free templates

Sign up for our free book summaries!
Inspire your next head-turning idea.
hcleadershipessentials.com/pages/book-summaries

LEADERSHIP ESSENTIALS
by HarperCollins Leadership

For more business and leadership advice and resources, visit hcleadershipessentials.com.

  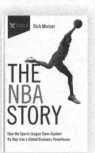